# THE MACHIAVELLIAN'S GUIDE TO *Flirting*

For Men *and* Women

by
Nick Casanova

iUniverse, Inc.
New York   Bloomington

The Machiavellian's Guide to Flirting
For Both Men and Women

iUniverse books may be ordered through booksellers or by contacting:

iUniverse
1663 Liberty Drive
Bloomington, IN 47403
www.iuniverse.com
1-800-Authors (1-800-288-4677)

Because of the dynamic nature of the Internet, any Web addresses or links contained in this book may have changed since publication and may no longer be valid. The views expressed in this work are solely those of the author and do not necessarily refl ect the views of the publisher, and the publisher hereby disclaims any responsibility for them.

This is a work of fiction. All of the characters, names, incidents, organizations, and dialogue in this novel are either the products of the author's imagination or are used fictitiously.

ISBN: 978-0-595-52607-9 (pbk)
ISBN: 978-0-595-62659-5 (ebk)

Printed in the United States of America

iUniverse rev. date 11/11/08

# Table of Contents

## FOR MEN

To Johnny and Rebecca: I hope you both lead long lives filled with opportunities to use these lines.

# Introduction

The key to being successful at love – apart from being good-looking and rich, neither of which this book can help you with – is to be playful: playfully suggestive, playfully romantic, and playfully bantering. In other words, you must know how to flirt.

Flirting is how you send the message that you're interested without saying so directly. If you are a skillful flirt, you can keep your prospect amused, giddy, titillated, flattered, and insulted all at the same time.

Flirting is also how you establish that you have a sense of humor, that you're smart, and that you're sane (without intelligence and sanity a sense of humor will not exist). And it's how you tell whether your prospect has those same qualities. Even if your prospect doesn't crack jokes himself, you can tell from his – or her -- reaction to yours whether or not he's socially aware and doesn't take himself too seriously. (It's also how you tell your prospect is a little lacking: dumb and/or pretentious people tend to make lame jokes.)

Unfortunately, in this age of internet-aided pickups, where people just list their sexual proclivities, flirting is something of a lost art. These days, many guys' idea of flirting is simply to ask, "Wanna hook up?" And many women's is to simply get breast implants. But this just makes flirting all the more devastating when it's done skillfully.

If someone has a crush on you to begin with, whatever you say will seem magical. This book will show you how to make your words *truly* magical.

We've all seen some famous actor interviewed and been struck by the thought, "Boy, is he stupid. He doesn't come across nearly as well as he does in the movies, and his comments are all so pedestrian." This is a simple fact of life: an actor without a script is a naked, helpless creature. Well, we are all actors on the stage of life, and we're never more likely to become tongue-tied than when with the object of our desire. In the face of beauty, many of us are simply struck dumb, in both senses of the term. So let this book be your script.

Please keep in mind that many of the strategies and lines recommended herein are playful in nature, so you must be sure that whomever you're flirting with is aware you are jesting. If she thinks you're serious when you're trying to be humorous, she'll think you ridiculous. If she thinks you serious when you're bantering, she'll consider you rude. But if both of you are in the right mood (just a trifle giddy), these routines can be great fun. (When the banter is really flowing, flirting can almost be more fun than sex itself.)

This book is divided into two sections, one for women and the other for men. You may notice that the "Banter" section is longer for women, while the "Be Romantic" section is longer for men, even though one might expect the opposite. This is by design. The whole point of this book is seduction – which means using whatever tactics work on the opposite sex. Men should be romantic, because that is what most women like, whereas women should banter more, because that is what men tend to enjoy. For the most part, every man's ideal woman thinks like a man, while every woman's ideal man is in touch with his feminine side.

One general rule of thumb for both sexes is, if you actually *feel* romantic about your paramour, no need to act that way. He (or she) will probably be aware of how you feel, and unless his feelings have been aroused to the same fever pitch, you don't want him to feel suffocated.

It used to be said that the way to a man's heart was through his stomach. It would be more accurate to say that the way is through his pride. The more implied compliments a woman's banter contains, the better; women never go too far wrong if they think of men as nothing more than walking egos.

With humans, as with the rest of the animal kingdom, it is usually the male who does the chasing and the female who does the choosing; these different roles lend themselves to different styles of flirting. (This statement does not pass the political correctness test, but flirting is by its nature a little improper.) Despite gender differences, however, most of the chapters (not all, but most) can be adapted for use by the opposite sex.

At the end of every chapter there is a hypothetical situation described, with a typical response from three types of people. The first is Mr. Inhibited (or Priss, in the case of females); we can all identify with this person at times. The second, more self-centered – and more off-putting -- response will come from a Hog (or Sow); this appellation refers not to appearance, only to behavior. Finally, we will hear from the Skillful Flirt. Mr. Inhibited (or the Priss) tend to be forgotten. Hogs and Sows tend to become roundly disliked. And Skillful Flirts tend to become romantically entwined.

The object of your desire will be referred to throughout the book as your "prospect." This is a term often used in sales, which is appropriate since flirting is all about selling yourself to your prospect.

There are those would call these tactics manipulative. They're right. But bear in mind that manipulation is least effective when recognizable as such. This book recommends tactics which generally are transparent only when meant to be.

Please take care to use these tactics only on the right people (those not given to taking offense) and at the right time (when both of you are in the mood). Many of the tactics described herein would backfire badly if used on the wrong people, or at the wrong time.

# Part A

## For Women

# Test the Waters

An initial feeling out process is necessary with any new prospect. Before you can actually start flirting, you need to find out if he is interested in you and if he's available. If he's attached, you need to fine out how tightly. And you also want to get some sense of what kind of boyfriend he'd make. But you mustn't ask any of those questions directly, for you might scare him off. Here are a few ways to find out while flattering him at the same time.

## Find out if He's Attached

The easiest way to ascertain your prospect's romantic status without appearing nosy is to act as if you simply assume he has a girlfriend.

For instance, if the conversation meanders within even a mile of the subject of relationships, casually comment, "You're obviously the type who's never without a girlfriend – or two."

Or, more flirtatiously, "I can't believe your girlfriend would let you come alone to a place like this where some strange woman might take advantage of you. I know I wouldn't let you out of my sight." (Just about any man will be pleased at the thought that there are women out there ready to pounce on him.)

Or, less flirtatiously, "Your girlfriend doesn't mind when you dress like that?"

If your prospect doesn't have a girlfriend, all of these comments will almost undoubtedly be met with "I don't have a girlfriend."

If you want to double check to see if he's telling the truth, or if you're looking for more details, answer, "I don't believe you." (Don't make it sound as if you're calling him a liar, rather as if you can't believe that a catch like him wouldn't have a girlfriend.) At this point he may feel obliged to shed a little more light on his love life, or lack thereof. Listen up.

**Situation**: You want to find out if your prospect is attached.

**Priss:** Doesn't ask, merely continues to wonder, hoping he will volunteer some clue.

**Sow:** "So, you gotta girlfriend or something?"

**Skillful Flirt:** "I bet your girlfriend likes you in that shirt. In fact I bet she even picked it out for you."

## "You Two Make Such a Cute Couple"

If you're curious as to the strength of the bond between your prospect and his girlfriend, certain comments will probably elicit a telling response.

Start by saying, "You're both so adorable." By making the comment about her as well as him, and using the word "adorable", which has a maternal ring to it, you keep it in the nonsexual realm. Yet the message that you think him attractive will be unmistakably communicated.

Then say, "You must be so happy to be with her." Or, alternatively, "She must be so happy to be with you." (If there is any discontent in Eden, it will probably be aired now.)

Ask, "Is she as nice as she seems?" (This is a fairly direct question disguised as a compliment.)

Or, "She is just perfect." (If she is anything less, this provides an opportunity for him to unload.)

"I bet the two of you end up getting married." Everybody knows that marriage will magnify the most trivial personality defect, the kind which can be overlooked in the throes of a hot and heavy affair, but which will acquire the ability to curdle milk over time. This will probably get him to give voice to his misgivings.

"I like the way you're so faithful to her." If he's not, he may be reluctant to disappoint you by telling you that he's not. But his expression may reveal the truth; observe carefully.

You can always say, "I'm jealous." This is a more direct statement than any you've made so far, but it's also interpretable as a harmless compliment.

At worst, after all these comments he will just file you away in his list of potential prospects, a list every guy keeps tucked away in some corner of his brain.

> **Situation:** You don't know how tight your prospect and his girlfriend are.
>
> **Priss:** Just assumes he is totally off-limits, and doesn't even make preliminary inquiries.
>
> **Sow:** "I just can't see you with her - she seems like such a bitch."
>
> **Skillful Flirt:** "Your girlfriend seems almost too good to be true...."

## "I Feel as if I Really Know You"

If there's a guy you've seen around whom you find attractive, but whom you barely know, a good way to break the ice is to give the following speech:

"You barely know me, but I have to tell you, I honestly feel as if I already know you; let me tell you why. I've seen that look of annoyance that passes over your face whenever you're around [an obnoxious mutual acquaintance], and I think to myself, I feel *exactly the same way*."

"I've seen the look of boredom you have at some of our indoctrination sessions." [This can be said of pretty much any school or corporation.] "And I have to say, again, I feel *exactly the same way*.

"And I've seen you barely able to suppress a smile as you listen to [a delusional mutual acquaintance]. And I'm reminded of how I have to laugh whenever I hear that idiot talk myself.

"So.....even though we've barely spoken, I somehow feel very..... *simpatico* with you."

The benefits of this approach are fivefold. First, he'll be flattered that you've noticed him. Second, it allows you to approach him in a friendly but not overtly sexual way. Third, it's always nice to know that someone understands you. Fourth, you'll have proved your intelligence (people always assume that someone with the same opinions as them is smart). And fifth, he'll think that since you seem to feel that you already know him, he'll have to waste less time on those getting-to-know-you preliminaries females always seem to insist on before they're ready for the good stuff, which will encourage him to pursue you.

---

**Situation:** You've been observing an attractive man who is part of your social milieu, but whom you don't really know very well.

**Priss:** Merely continues to observe, pining away from a distance.

**Sow:** Thrusts her breasts in his face and very suggestively purrs "Hi!"

**Skillful Flirt:** Appearing to be forcing herself to do so, hesitantly goes up to him and "shyly" gives the above speech.

---

## "You're Probably Just the Love 'em and Leave 'em Type"

If you want to get a sense of how you're going to be treated by a prospective beau, and possibly flatter him at the same time, dismiss him as a heartless cad and see how he reacts. If he smilingly agrees with you, you can dismiss him permanently, unless that's what you're looking for. If he protests, however, he's either a nice guy or a liar. (You can judge which by the rest of his conversation.)

So sound him out about that; given the teasing nature of your comments, he'll never know he's being tested:

"I see you as the slam-bam-thank-you-ma'am type."

"You probably have notches on your bedpost to commemorate all your sexual escapades."

"I get the sense that you see women more as conquests than as people."

"You probably have no problem dumping girls after you're through with them. You just say 'See you later', right?"

"You're probably the kind of guy who, after making love to a girl, never bothers to spend the night."

"I'm guessing your love life is pretty much like an assembly line."

His response – or lack thereof – will give you some sense of the kind of man you're dealing with.

> **Situation:** You're trying to feel out a prospective suitor.
>
> **Priss:** "I'm trying to figure out if you're a nice guy."
>
> **Sow:** "You seem like you'd be a really lousy boyfriend."
>
> **Skillful Flirt:** "You're probably the type who, once he's scored, just puts his clothes on and walks out the door without another word. Am I right?"

# Let Him Know You're Attracted

It has been said that everybody makes an important judgment within the first few seconds of meeting someone of the opposite sex, namely, if they would want to have sex with that person. This may not rise to the level of a conscious decision, but everyone is aware of their own decision, consciously or not. And they are aware that a similar decision has been made about them. Thus, you need to let your prospect know that he has not just passed the test, but done so with honors.

## "I Bet You're a Real Heartbreaker"

There's nothing a man likes to hear more than that you consider him attractive enough to be a real Lothario, so indulge him.

"I bet you have girls throwing themselves at you left and right."

When your prospect demurs, act as if you assume he's lying: "Oh please. I'm sure you have an entire harem at your disposal."

"It's obvious you're the kind of man who cuts a pretty wide swath. I bet you have a girlfriend in every town in this county."

"I bet most girls are just like fish in a barrel for you."

The implication of all these comments is that you yourself are attracted to him, otherwise you wouldn't assume that other women are.

If he continues to demur, ask, "Have you ever looked in a mirror? You *know* you're attractive. I'm sure you can get any girl you want."

This will evoke an image of all the girls he wanted but couldn't get (most guys have a pretty long list), so he will probably say that that's not true. Reply, "Well even if you had your heart broken once or twice, I'm sure you've broken hundreds in turn. Most of them you probably didn't even know about." He may be aware of one or two girls he's hurt, but he'll find the idea that there are hundreds of girls he's left heartbroken and didn't even know about extremely flattering.

The thought of all that foregone potential sex will also make him want to make up for lost time – which will make him even easier to manipulate.

**Situation:** You're at a party, and someone says to both of you that your prospect is very popular with the ladies.

**Priss:** "Oh?"

**Sow:** (after giving him the once over and thoughtfully pursing her lips): "Nah. I don't see it."

**Skillful Flirt:** "Of course he is. Look at him."

# "You're So Vain"

This was the title of a famous song by Carly Simon, who wrote it with a poison pen. But if you listen to the words of the song closely, you'll realize that most guys – superficial as they are -- actually wouldn't mind being the fellow she was singing to. (The implicit assumption is that he had quite a bit to be vain about.) And while Carly used a bitter tone, you can use a flirtatious one:

"Boy, you really strut around like you're God's gift to women, don't you?" (The implication, of course, is that he is.)

"I bet you're so proud of those cheekbones of yours." (Use whatever he's proud of, be it his forearms or jacket or car – he'll be happy you noticed.)

"Why is it that guys with big arms have to wear muscle shirts all the time?"

"Look at you with those tight pants, the better to show off those cute little buns."

"You must put a lot of effort into making your hair look so carelessly tousled."

"I bet you're the kind of guy who just gazes lovingly into every reflective surface he sees."

"Why don't you just get a t-shirt printed up with [the accomplishment of which he's most proud] written on it?"

"Your middle name must be Conceit. You're so vain you probably thought that song was about *you*."

The main benefit of this approach is that implies that your prey has a lot to be vain about, which he'll find quite pleasing.

> **Situation:** You catch your handsome prospect looking at himself in a mirror. What do you say?
>
> **Priss:** (Nothing.)
>
> **Sow:** (in a voice dripping with disgust) "You must be really insecure."
>
> **Skillful Flirt:** "You really should just carry around a little hand mirror so that you can just admire yourself whenever the mood strikes you.

## "Let Me Just Drink in Your Features"

At pretty much any point in your courtship, in fact at just about any point in any conversation, you can say, "Wait....." and then use the above line. Its effect is never less than extremely flattering.

Say, "Forgive me, but I just enjoy staring at you so much. Your face is just so....stare-able at."(Sometimes the message is more memorable when you use a word which doesn't exist, and you come across more sincere when less eloquent.)

"You know, I try to close my eyes and picture your face when I'm not with you, but after I've imagined it a certain number of times, I can't bring the image forth anymore. So let me just memorize it again."

"You must be used to people just gawking at you. Do you consider it a pain?"

"Sorry – is it rude for me to just gaze at you like this? If it is, I'll *try* to stop. I just don't know that I'll succeed."

"You know, Tolstoy once said, 'It is amazing how complete the illusion that beauty is goodness.' I can see how true that is right now. For all I know you're a devil, but you certainly look like an angel."

"What's amazing is that every single one of your features is just right. With most people, you can see their flaws right off. But with you, I wouldn't change a single thing. If you went to a plastic surgeon, he'd probably just say, 'Sorry, there's nothing I can do to improve you'."

**Situation:** Your prospect kiddingly asks you to please stop staring at him.

**Priss:** (too mortified to realize it's a joke) "Oh, sorry."

**Sow:** (ignoring the fact that it's a joke so she can wax self-righteous) "You're going to tell me where I can look now? Jesus, are you controlling."

**Skillful Flirt:** (ignoring the fact that it's a joke so she can flatter him) "Sorry, normally I don't do that. It's strange, but I actually feel a little drunk just from looking at you."

## "Good-looking Guys Always Think…"

If you want to flatter your prospect without seeming to be trying to do so, criticize his actions by saying something along the lines of, "Why is it good-looking guys always think they can get away with that kind of behavior?"

No matter what he does, interpret it in that light:

"Good-looking guys always seem to think they don't have to do things like hold the door open for somebody else."

"Good-looking guys always just assume that other people are going to be happy to do them favors."

"There's nothing worse than a handsome guy who's been spoiled by all the attention he gets from girls."

"Good-looking guys are always doing things like borrowing things and never returning them."

"I have yet to meet a good-looking guy who can cook."

Say all these things in a tone of exasperated (but not bitter) disapproval. Don't worry: after each "criticism" he will glow. After all, being told he's good-looking far outweighs the fact that he forgot to hold the door open one time or neglected to return something. Yet if each complaint is phrased as a nominal disapproval, it won't come across as if you're *trying* to butter him up. And you might even get him to improve his behavior, at least temporarily.

**Situation:** You're having dinner with your prospect and he refills his own wine glass but not yours.

**Priss:** "Could I have some more too please?"

**Sow:** "You pig! You refill your own wine glass but not mine?! I can't believe how selfish you are!"

**Skilled Flirt:** "I guess guys as handsome as you never bother with the social niceties because they basically don't have to."

## "You Should be Ashamed, Flaunting Yourself Like That"

These days, accusations of shamelessness sound a bit quaint. Yet there's still a slight stigma of disapproval attached to those who parade themselves around in skimpy clothing. Nonetheless, this is a temptation that many with great bodies – and many without – succumb to. So go ahead and be the voice of Puritanical disapproval -- as long as your prospect knows you're not entirely serious. He'll enjoy the implicit compliment him on his great body.

"Could those clothes be any tighter?"

"My but you're proud of that body, aren't you?"

"If you really want to show off your body that badly, why don't you just come to work in a Speedo?"

"You dress as if you're performing at Chippendale's – and you're about halfway through your routine."

"If you've got it, flaunt it, right? I guess shame isn't really part of your emotional repertoire, is it?"

"You look like a parade of sex walking by."

"You know what message you're sending with that outfit, don't you -- look at me?"

> **Situation:** Your prospect is wearing a tight t-shirt and form-fitting jeans.
>
> **Stiff:** Just stares, then, when caught looking, looks away quickly, as if she's the one who should be ashamed.
>
> **Sow:** "You'd look right at home in a gay bar."
>
> **Skillful Flirt:** "I guess there's really no point in working out if you don't get to display the results."

## "You Know What My Friends and I Call You?"

To multiply the value of any compliment, attribute it to a group of people by saying that they all refer to your prospect by the same flattering nickname. Just make sure it fits.

The best nicknames, of course, are those which refer to his appearance:

"Do you know what we all call you? Adonis."

Say he's referred to as Pitt, Clooney, Depp, or whichever movie star he resembles.

Choosing a character from a movie rather than the star himself is even better (he gets all the heroic qualities of the fictional character without any of the moronic qualities of the actor himself): "Indiana Jones", or "Luke Skywalker", "Aragorn", or "Legolas".

Or you can just say that your friends all refer to him as "Hollywood," which conveys vague connotations of glamour without highlighting the fact that he's an inferior version of some star.

If he's built, say, "We call you 'The Body'." Or, on a slightly more subtle note, "Speedo." (No one would call someone that just because he wears them; he would have to look good in them.)

If he's smart, say that your friends all refer to him as Einstein. Or Sherlock Holmes.

If he seems tough, or, more to the point, cares about being tough, use "Blood and Guts." Or "The Terminator."

You can be pretty sure that your prospect won't check with your friends to see if you're telling the truth, but just in case he meets some of them and the subject comes up, you might want to use the monicker with your friends one or two times, even if you must do so sarcastically.

If you really want to flatter your prospect, tell him your friends call him "James Bond." This combines looks, glamour, and savoir-faire with a license to slay the ladies.

**Situation:** You're telling your prospect what your friends think of him.

**Priss:** "Most of them don't really know you that well."

**Sow:** (Most like him, and have said so, but one once said she thought he was a little conceited.) "They think you're conceited."

**Skillful Flirt:** "Know what we all call you? Tarzan."

## "You're Better-Looking Than Him"

Most guys, unless totally egocentric, will express admiration for another guy at some point. When your prospect does so, immediately throw the compliment back at him.

When he says, "Peter is so smart," reply, "You're just as smart," in a tone that indicates a slight exasperation that he doesn't see this. Intelligence is a nebulous quality that most imagine they possess more of than they do, so he may believe you.

When he says, "Brian is so strong," reply, "You're as strong as him." If the difference is painfully obvious, insert the word "almost" into your statement. Your claim may be obviously untrue. But the mere fact that you've said it will make him *feel* strong, and after all, you're only trying to get him to puff his chest out a bit.

No matter what quality he expresses admiration for, immediately give him the same plaudits. He will be forever grateful to you – even if he doesn't realize it. The more intangible the quality, the better. It's hard to tell someone that their accomplishments are just as good ("But you're an Olympic champion too").

Looks are a particularly fertile field for this sort of compliment. If your prospect says hat he wishes he looked as good as so-and-so, simply tell him that he does. The one compliment that people always remember is when they're told they're good-looking. Other compliments tend to disappear down the memory hole, but unless someone is extraordinarily handsome, being told he is so is something he will treasure for years.

**Situation:** Your prospect says, "Wow, Jim is just so cool."

**Priss:** "He is."

**Sow:** "Yeah, he's the opposite of you."

**Skillful Flirt:** "Oh puh-lease. You're cooler than him."

# "You Could be a Gigolo"

If you really want to put visions of sugar plums in your prospect's head, tell him he could be a gigolo if he wanted to be. The idea that women would actually pay him for his services is, of course, absolutely delightful for just about any guy.

Say, "I know plenty of women who would pay you to be their escort.... I bet a lot of them would think it would enhance their status to be seen with a guy who looks like you."

A variation on this theme is, "You could be a male model." This sends pretty much the same message.

But it's sexier to stick with the prostitution angle: "I'm serious. You could make a decent living just being a high class gigolo." This is of course wildly unrealistic, but, men being inclined to egotism, he will probably believe you.

When a man becomes convinced of his attractive powers to the opposite sex, the level of pheromones in the air goes up about threefold.

**Situation:** Your prospect, a good-looking college junior, is fretting about what he's going to do for a living after he graduates.

**Priss:** "I know, me too."

**Sow:** "You could always be a hustler, you know, have guys pay you for sex."

**Skillful Flirt:** "Are you kidding? If you wanted to you could just be a gigolo…."

# Play to His Ego

If you can stroke your prospect in the secret place where he most wants stroking, he will become putty in your hands. That place, of course, is his ego. The extent to which men think with their egos cannot be overestimated. In other words, they can be egotistical about every last aspect of their lives, things you'd never guess they are touchy about – or proud of. They pretty much walk, talk, eat, sleep, and breathe with their egos. You needn't necessarily give your prospect compliments; just paying attention to him can sometimes do the trick. (And the more insecure he is, the more easily you can manipulate him.)

Remember, most men are so desperate for praise they will easily become addicted to your compliments, and, by extension, to you.

## Hang on His Every Word

What have we all wanted from the time we were small? To be the center of attention. When we're young, we're uninhibited about asking for attention, but by the time we're adults we've been socialized not to. Deep down, though, we still crave it. Ergo, by giving your prey your undivided attention, you fulfill his deepest desire. The key word here is "undivided." Think of those snake charmers who never let their gaze waver from the cobra's.

People who've been with the great seducers often say afterward that they were made to feel that they were the only person in the world who mattered at that particular moment. This has been said about Warren Beatty, Bill Clinton, and Pamela Harriman, among others. Simply focus on your prey with laser-like intensity. (The obnoxious person does the opposite, gazing distractedly around the room.)

Even if your prospect is droning on about the Yankees' season, or some other topic you find utterly dreary, gaze at him as if he were foretelling your future.

Nod frequently, and wear a look of slight awe, as if what he is saying is the crystallization of all that you have vaguely felt but have never quite been able to put into such cogent form.

By feigning entrancement, you will entrance your prospect. By pretending to be under a magical spell, you are in fact casting one.

Eventually, your prospect will realize, if only subconsciously, that you will provide the attention he craves, and he will come to need you the way a junkie needs his fix.

The best part about this technique is that it requires no special talent on your part, other than, as the old joke goes, being a good listener.

> **Situation:** Your prospect is droning on about the local real estate market.
>
> **Priss:** Can't help but let her gaze wander from time to time.
>
> **Sow:** "Seriously, who gives a shit?"
>
> **Skillful Flirt:** (regretfully) "Listening to you talk really makes me wish I had a tape recorder."

## "You're Such a Showoff"

If you happen to see your prospect in his natural athletic habitat, i.e., playing his main sport, you can both compliment and gently tease him at the same time by accusing him of showing off. If he's courting you, he may have arranged to play you at whatever sport he's good at in order to do exactly that, so he probably deserves whatever abuse you give him. If he's not showing off, and he's not even very good, accuse him anyway. (Feeling like a strutting rooster is not an unpleasant sensation).

Let's say he played collegiate tennis, and he's generously offered to have a match with you. Once he has started to trounce you, feel free to playfully ask any of the following questions:

"Was there any reason for asking me to play other than to just show how good you are?"

"Is this part of your normal routine with a girl – dragging her to the court so you can establish your superiority?"

"So you wanted a good match, eh? Are you always this transparent or do you ever hide it better?"

"Do you ever play with people at your own level or do you just prefer to just beat mediocre players like me?"

"Do you ever stop showing off?"

All these questions simultaneously flatter him and put him on the spot, which is the essence of flirtation.

---

**Situation:** A top swimmer has invited you to the pool for a "fun swim", but then he proceeds to demonstrate his butterfly under the pretext of "getting a little workout as long as I'm here."

**Priss:** "You're good at that."

**Sow:** "I guess you think you're really hot stuff."

**Skillful Flirt:** "You must hate having to go to sleep every night and be unable to show off for eight entire hours."

---

## "You're So Macho"

Another way to flirt is to tease your prospect about his maleness in such a way that shows you consider machismo silly, but at the same time are aware and appreciative of his overwhelming masculinity:

"You seem to have too much testosterone for your own good.....You ever think about taking some estrogen just to calm you down a little?"

"When you feel your honor has been slighted, do you challenge another man to a duel? Or do you just beat him up on the spot?"

"Are you part gorilla?"

"I bet you like to drive your car real fast and play music loudly, don't you?"

"I bet they had a hard time civilizing you."

"You strike me as the type of guy who'd be into extreme sports."

"So what do you eat for breakfast, railroad spikes?"

"I'm guessing you're one of those guys who has to shave twice a day."

"Your poor girlfriends, I bet you demand sex from them all the time."

You get the idea. Even if he's a lamb, make him feel like a lion.

---

**Situation:** You're looking at a stack of magazines on your prospect's coffee table. (He has Sports Illustrated, GQ, and Time.)

**Priss:** Says nothing, just looks at them.

**Sow:** "So where do you keep the Hustlers, under your bed?"

**Skillful Flirt:** "Hmm. I'd figured a guy like you would be more into Soldier of Fortune or Guns & Ammo."

---

## "You're So Worldly"

Some men like to be thought macho, others prefer to be thought worldly (actually, most like to be thought both). In any case, all men are pathetic creatures who can be easily reached via their egos. So if your prospect's primary pretensions are those of sophistication, indulge him.

You may remember the song, *I Am Fifteen Going on Sixteen* from *The Sound of Music*. Oscar Hammerstein, who knew his way around a set of lyrics, was particularly skillful at creating a romantic mood. The gist of this song was that Liesl was – in her words – a mere innocent compared to Hans, her seventeen-old beau. This sentiment might not pass muster with feminists, but it will warm the hearts of most men, since it will give them the (false) feeling of having the upper hand.

So if your prospect demonstrates any knowledge at all about wines, or cigars, or the stock market, or jazz, or anything, marvel at his savoir-faire: "Wow – I know nothing at all about literature. You're really a man of the world, aren't you?"

"I'd never come to a restaurant like this on my own. But I can tell, this is just routine for you, isn't it?"

"And how do you happen to now so much about brandies? You've really been around, haven't you?" The "been around" phraseology has sexual implications – but that's okay, since no man will be displeased by the assumption that he has had lots of women.

Even if your prospect is just a sheep ready for the shearing, give him credit for more experience that he has, and act as if you are just a starry-eyed ingénue agog at his sophistication.

**Situation:** Your prospect refills your glass of wine.

**Priss:** "Thank you."

**Sow:** Not wanting to pass up free wine, just picks it up and drains it, then sets it down in front of him again.

**Skillful Flirt:** "You seem so at home in this fancy restaurant. I just feel so naïve by comparison."

## "Your Mind is So Agile"

If your prospect is a wit, or fancies himself one, do not discourage him:

"You have the most amazing mind. I've never met anyone like you. The way you think – it's incredible!" Very few people have enough perspective on themselves to know that this is not true.

"Listening to you talk is like being at a Noel Coward play."

"I could just sit here and listen to you talk forever."

"You have a comeback for everything. I could never win a battle of wits with you."

On a slightly more negative note: "You should be a politician the way you can twist things around."

"You can just come at a person from all sorts of angles. You feint, you counterpunch, and you throw combinations. You're the Sugar Ray Leonard of conversation."

"I think the secret to your charm is that you can identify with all sorts of people. Most of us pretty much can only identify with ourselves, but you seem to always know what's going on inside other peoples' minds."

"I think that rather than just having a dialogue with you, I'd prefer to listen to you play my part as well. *I'd* get better lines that way, that's for sure. You could be a great playwright if you wanted to."

---

**Situation:** Your prospect finishes your sentences for you, saying just what you were going to say.

**Priss:** "That's exactly what I was going to say!"

**Sow:** "Will you ever let me get a word in edgewise?"

**Skillful Flirt:** "It's amazing the way you anticipate everything I say. I feel as if I just learned how to play chess and I'm competing against a grandmaster."

---

## "You're Different from All the Other Boys around Here"

You can always make your prospect feel special by telling him that he's different from everybody else in town. You needn't even specify exactly what you mean by that; vague compliments are always welcome, and almost always interpreted as positively as possible.

So just say, "You're not like all the other people around here, are you?" (No one will ever disagree with this.)

"Everyone else around here is sort of a clone. But not you." (Since everybody sees himself as different, but notices similarities between others, he will tend to agree.)

"You seem more sensitive than the rest of the guys around here." (No one ever thinks of himself as *in*sensitive.)

"I've never met anybody quite like you before." (Guys being guys, they will inevitably interpret this as a compliment, though it could be construed either way.)

"You're such a breath of fresh air. Most of the guys around here are so dull."

"You're one of a kind." (Humans are indeed like snowflakes that way.)

"What I like about you is, you're not just one of the crowd. You march to your own drummer."

**Situation:** You're trying to tell your prospect what you like about him.

**Priss:** "You're always polite and stuff."

**Sow:** "I've seen you in gym shorts, I can tell you're well hung."

**Skillful Flirt:** "I'm so glad you're not just another typical product of our hometown. Most of the guys around here, it's like they were all taught the same set of opinions, sayings, and jokes. At least you can think for yourself."

## "Something about Your Self-Assurance is Incredibly Sexy"

Self-confidence is one of those intangible qualities that everybody seems to define differently. If you tell your prospect that he has it, he will find some way to see the "truth" of your statement.

Tell him, "You know how women always say that they like a guy with self-confidence? You seem to be one of those guys."

"I like the way you're self-confident without swaggering. The guys who swagger, I always get the impression they've got something to prove."

"You have a quiet self-confidence about you. It's as if you have this inner calm from knowing your own worth as a human being."

"You're probably aware of this, but your body language makes a real statement – that you have an inner calm. I can tell because you're not a fidgeter."

"I like the way you're comfortable in your own skin. Most guys aren't, you know. They're always trying to prove something."

"There's something about the way you stretch and move your head that's just so relaxed it's very appealing."

There's a side benefit to this approach: by telling him he's self-confident, you'll actually make him more so.

**Situation:** Your prospect strides into the room.

**Priss:** "Hi John."

**Sow:** "Well look who's here -- the self-proclaimed king of the world."

**Skillful Flirt:** "You know, the way you walk just projects self-confidence. It's as if…you just know you're in control somehow. I mean, other people make more noise, but you don't have to."

## "You Really Think about Things"

Everybody's brain, no matter how low the wattage, is always at work in some way or another, and few people realize that their ideas are no good. So give your prospect credit where he thinks it is due:

"One thing about you, I can tell you've always got something working upstairs."

"Judging from the glint in your eye, I know you're thinking about *something* bad." (Say this with a glint in your own eye.)

Look at him bemusedly and say, "Those wheels are always turning, aren't they?"

"I wish I could read your mind. I know there are a lot of interesting thoughts up there."

"You really ponder things, don't you? I mean a lot of guys seem to just stumble through life on auto-pilot, but you really examine it, don't you?"

"I can tell you're the type who's always thinking. When you set your mind to a problem, you don't stop till you've really solved it."

"You're never *not* thinking, are you? I honestly think your brain works about twice as fast as most peoples'."

**Situation:** Your prospect is gazing off into space distractedly.

**Priss:** Worries that she has done something to offend him.

**Sow:** "Boy are you a barrel of laughs."

**Skillful Flirt:** "Look at you. I bet you're thinking some pretty weighty thoughts there. So what are you thinking about, physics or calculus?"

## Meaningless Compliments

Flattery which has little basis in fact is still nice to hear. And if a compliment is impossible to prove, that makes it ipso facto impossible to disprove as well:

"You're sweet."

"You're cool."

"You're neat."

"You're my favorite."

"You have undeniable sex appeal."

"You're the best."

"You're amazing."

"You're very appealing."

"You're cute."

"You're adventurous."

"You *have* something."

"You're great."

It would be extremely egotistical for your prospect to ask, "How am I great?" But if he does (and no one ever went broke underestimating the vanity of men), you can always reply, in similarly obtuse fashion, "I don't know, you just are."

**Situation:** You and your prospect arrange to meet on a certain street corner at noon. He is on time, you are five minutes late. What do you say?

**Priss:** "Sorry I'm late."

**Sow:** "Good. I was afraid you'd be late." (Annoyance seeps into her voice at the very thought that he might have kept her waiting.)

**Skillful Flirt:** "I know I can always depend on you."

## "The First Time I Saw You"

Your prospect will get a kick out of it if you had some sort of egregiously erroneous impression of him when you first saw him. This is a game usually played once people have already become lovers, but there's no reason you can't move the timetable up in an effort to achieve that status.

You can make the comment as flattering or as insulting as you want it to be, since you can't be held responsible for your initial impression, especially since the only reason you'd be telling him this in the first place is to show how wrong you were. So tell him:

"I thought you were some kind of real tough guy."

"I figured you for a spoiled rich kid."

"I thought you were gay."

"I thought you were some kind of criminal."

"I thought you were autistic, the way you rarely spoke to people."

No matter what you say your impression was, it will be flattering simply because you remember the first time you saw him, something we usually don't do with people who do not make an impression on us.

**Situation:** Your prospect tells you he was struck by your looks the first time he saw you.

**Priss:** "Oh thanks."

**Sow:** "I don't remember the first time I saw you."

**Skillful Flirt:** "I thought you were one of these super-sophisticated types who look down on everyone else. I figured you'd never talk to someone like me."

## "You're an Interesting Guy"

If you want to tell your prospect that you're interested in him without being that direct, tell him he's "interesting", which almost always translates as "I'm interested."

If you say, "You're one of the most interesting people I know," it's a nice compliment.

If you change that to "You're one of the most interesting guys I know," that translates as, "I'm open to the possibilities here."

If you change that to, "You're the most interesting guy I've ever met," that translates fairly directly as, "Let's do it – now." (But since you're not saying it in those words, it's acceptable.)

So, whenever he tells a story, no matter how dull, comment, "That's interesting." (Follow this comment up with a question, to show you actually are interested.)

"You always have your own take on a situation."

If he relates an anecdote that's mildly interesting, stare at him and say, "That's fascinating." (Take care not to sound sarcastic.)

"I could just sit and listen to you forever."

A related comment is, "I love the sound of your voice." (The implication is, "The vibrations from your basso profundo go straight to my G spot.")

**Situation:** Your prospect tells you a moderately interesting story.

**Priss:** "Oh. I didn't know that."

**Sow:** "That story was way too long for how interesting it was."

**Skillful Flirt:** "You are amazing. You have more interesting stories than anyone I know."

## "You Know All the Right Moves, Don't You?"

If your prospect is in need of encouragement – as so many men are – give him credit for playing the game well. Whatever his actual ability at seduction, act tickled to have come across such a pro:

"You just know exactly which buttons to push, don't you?"

"You're an old hand at this game, aren't you?"

"You know all the cute little things to say."

"I bet the girls just wet their pants thinking about how adorable you are."

"You're a veritable master of manipulation. I can feel myself being swayed as we speak."

"You're awfully slick."

"You could write a book on how to pick up women."

Sound a little wistful as you say these things, as if you are resigned to the fact that it's probably your fate to be just another notch on his bedpost

> **Situation:** Your prospect says he enjoys dancing and executes a little shimmy and twist to emphasize his point.
>
> **Priss:** Half stifles a laugh.
>
> **Sow:** "You're really quite taken with yourself, aren't you?"
>
> **Skillful Flirt:** "To be confident enough to pull off a move like that, you must have had a lot of success with women.....That was actually pretty cool – can you do it again?"

## "My Read on You…"

You can captivate your prospect early on by telling him that you've got him figured out. It helps to be a good reader of people – most fortunetellers have this skill – but even if you're not, at least you'll be talking about him, and it's a fairly safe bet that's his favorite topic of discussion anyway. So say something along the following lines (choose one of each set, depending):

"You seem a little spoiled, so I'm guessing you're an only child." *Or*, "You seem to be able to get along well with people, so I'm guessing you came from a large family."

"You're careful with your money, so I take it you didn't come from a rich family." *Or*, "You're a bit of a spendthrift, so I gather money was never a problem when you were growing up."

"You seem very trusting, and that usually means that you came from a loving family." *Or*, "You seem a bit mistrustful, and that often means a difficult childhood."

"You're obviously athletic, and judging from your build I'm going to guess swimming or wrestling." *Or*, "You probably find sports a little boring and childish, and look down your nose at jocks."

"Judging from your vocabulary and syntax, you probably went to good schools." *Or*, "You have far too much common sense to have spent much time in college."

"Judging from your dress, you're quite ambitious and sophisticated." *Or*, "Your clothes say that you're a laid back sort of guy who's secure enough not to have to advertise himself that way."

The beauty of a field like astrology is that most people can seem themselves in every description. The same goes for these lines. And even if you do get some disagreement, you'll score points for having dwelled on his favorite subject for a while.

## Calmly Analyze Him

There's something very sexy about someone who can see right through you. If you can pick apart your prospect's every action, he might just become putty in your hands. It's also a great way to put him on the defensive. Your analysis need not be insulting; but it should be accurate. (This chapter is more analysis after the fact, whereas the previous one was more about initial conjecture.)

If your prospect affects a wholesome manner, and actually succeeds in coming across like the boy next door, tell him, "That 'aw shucks' routine works well for you." (Characterizing his persona as a "routine" shows a nice, dryly cynical touch.)

If he loses his temper, say, 'Being temperamental like that must really work at keeping others on the defensive." (Keep in mind, you need a very good reason to want to have a temperamental type as your prospect.)

If he's modest, say, "That self-deprecating act goes down real smooth. I can tell you've practiced it a lot."

If he ever convinces anyone to do something he wants, say, "That was really slick the way you manipulated that guy into doing what you wanted. You're quite the operator, aren't you?"

If he's boastful (most men are, whether they do it subtly or unsubtly), say, "My, but you have an ego, don't you? Tell me, what percent of people act impressed by you, and what percent try to one-up you?"

If he uses a lot of lines that have a used quality to them, say, "You have a lot of prepackaged routines, don't you? Tell me, how many times have you used that particular line?"

> **Situation:** Your prospect compliments you on your appearance.
>
> **Priss:** "Thank you."
>
> **Sow:** "I hear that a lot."
>
> **Skillful Flirt:** "You're a very skillful flatterer. Do you ever actually mean it?"

## "I Like Your Self Control"

Self-control is another intangible quality that everyone feels he has, even if he does not. So indulge your prospect and tell him:

"I have to admire your will power. You're going to go far in life, I can tell."

"I wish I were as disciplined as you. I'm afraid I let myself go sometimes. But you – you stick to your plans."

"I like the way you do what you want to do." (Who doesn't do this?)

"You don't give in to every whim." (None of us can afford to do that.)

At this point, shift the conversation to the idea that he should relax a little more:

"And you seem to be in control of your emotions. You never let them get the better of you. Sometimes I wonder if you're not a little too tightly wound, like a volcano that's been dormant for too long."

"I'm a little worried about you. I'm afraid that when you finally blow, it's going to be a big explosion."

"Don't you ever feel the urge to just let loose, be a little dissolute?" (This is the path you want to lead your prospect down.)

You know, you only live once." If he's young, say, "You're only young once." (These thoughts tend to lead to self-indulgence.)

**Situation:** Your prospect tells you that he doesn't want to go to a party tonight because   he's got football practice the next morning.

**Priss:** "Okay."

**Sow:** "That's absolutely pathetic."

**Skillful Flirt:** "I'm sure your coach appreciates your dedication, but it does seem you're wasting your life that way."

## "I'm Going to Be Impossible to Live with"

If your prospect has been generous with his compliments, tell him, "You've been a very bad influence on me. You've pretty much turned me into a raving egomaniac. Nobody else can stand to be around me anymore -- but at least I'm enjoying myself."

"I just go around repeating your compliments to everyone: 'I know this really cool guy who told me…'."

"Whenever any of my friends ask me why I'm so conceited these days, I just tell them it's your fault, that you made me this way. My friends tell me that those are just lines, and that you're just saying these things because you want to get into my pants. But I tell them no, that you really mean them….. Anyway, if it *is* all lies, please don't tell me, okay, because I'm enjoying them too much."

By telling your prospect these things, you're showing him three things: first, that you have remembered his compliments, which is flattering to him. Secondly, you're telling him that he hasn't really turned your head and that you have your feet planted firmly on the ground. Thirdly, you're letting him know that you understand the game he's playing. (You're not necessarily expressing disapproval of the game, you're just letting him know you're onto him.)

So go on in this vein a bit: "I used to be modest, you know. But no longer. All your flattery has gone straight to my head. If pride is a sin, then I'm a sinner."

The overriding message you're sending here is that you've taken notice of him and his comments.

> **Situation:** Your prospect says you look really good for the third time.
>
> **Priss:** "I don't think so. But thank you anyway."
>
> **Sow:** "I know."
>
> **Skillful Flirt:** "You better watch out, or I'm going to develop an ego like a guy. I'll just be boasting all the time. Hey, why should guys have all the fun?"

# Play Coy

At times it is more fun – and even more titillating for your prospect – if you feign a complete lack of interest in your prospect. Men by nature generally prefer to chase than to be chased, and we all want what we can't have. So if you play hard to get, he will want to get you more. That's just human nature.

Of course, you can also do so playfully – in a way which sends the opposite message. (No one would ever bother to tell someone else that they weren't interested in him unless they were.) You must take care to be playful when doing this, so he doesn't interpret your comments as outright rejection. And remember, you can only follow these tactics with someone who is relatively secure, i.e., who can take a joke.

## "You Must Think I'm in Love with You"

There are times when the air is so full of pheromones that there is nothing for it but to deny them. Although these lines are mostly teasingly insulting, the underlying message is that you do like him, otherwise you wouldn't be taking this playful tone with him.

So, if your prospect accuses you of having fallen for him, respond, "You really have your head in the clouds, don't you?"

"Do you ever wake up or do you just live in dreamland all the time?"

"Are you so insecure that you actually have to invent reasons to be proud of yourself?"

"I'm happy for you that you have such a high opinion of yourself, I really am, but you ought to try sticking with reality."

"Have you ever been tested for schizophrenia?"

"I hate to clue you in, but you're not exactly my type. I like guys who are [list some traits he lacks]."

"Let me explain something. I don't get crushes on guys. It's not my nature. I consider men to be playthings, petty amusements. And you're barely even that."

"If all the guys in the world were like you, I'd probably turn into a lesbian."

"If you held a gun to my head while attempting to rape me, I'd probably just tell you to pull the trigger."

**Situation:** Your prospect accuses you of having a mad crush on him.

**Priss:** "Well, maybe just a little."

**Sow:** "If I were really horny and locked in a room with you and a snake, I'd still have a hard time choosing which of you to fuck."

**Skillful Flirt:** "You could feed me that date rape drug and I'd still be able to resist you."

## "I'd Hate to be Your Girlfriend"

If you want to put the idea into your prospect's head that you could be his girlfriend, mention that you wouldn't want to be his girlfriend. You needn't come up with any truly personal reasons, just the standard litany of complaints that women have about men:

"I sure wouldn't want to be your girlfriend, you'd just want sex all the time."

"You're handsome but you seem like the kind of guy who'd rather watch football than have sex."

"I'm guessing you'd be a horrible boyfriend, the type who'd just want to show me off to all his friends and then boast about how he has sex with me all the time. No thanks."

"I'd hate to date you, you seem the type who'd never admit he was wrong about anything and would get angry with me if I ever disagreed about anything."

"I might consider you as boyfriend material, except for the fact that you probably beat your girlfriends."

"You come in a cute package, I have to admit, it's just too bad you're so controlling. I bet you'd be the type to tell me how to dress and act in every situation."

"I don't know if I could ever trust you. You've got too much dog in you. Oh, and if I gained even two pounds, that would probably be the end."

Always say these things with a twinkle in your eye, just to let him know you don't really mean it.

Each time you tell your prospect how much you'd hate being his girlfriend, a little message will be sent to his subconscious saying, "She could be my girlfriend." His subconscious will then send the message "She'd be fun to fool around with" to his conscious brain.

A side benefit to this approach is that you can warn him about behaviors he'd better stay away from should you actually get involved.

**Situation:** Your prospect beats you at a game of Scrabble.

**Priss:** "I'm usually not this bad."

**Sow:** "What a stupid game."

**Skillful Flirt:** I feel sorry for your girlfriends, you're probably the type of boyfriend who has to beat them at everything." Gives a mock shudder.

## "I Wouldn't Want to Encourage You"

If you want to encourage a reluctant swain, but not blatantly, just say you don't want to. The following lines must be delivered saucily, with a hint of humor. If you come across harsh, your prospect might take you at your word.

"I'd be friendlier to you, but you might get the wrong idea."

"I'd suggest getting a cup of coffee sometime, but I think I'm going to refrain, because that would probably make you think I'm interested in dating you."

"I have to be very careful with you not to give the wrong impression, because you'll get all sorts of ideas about me being available, which I'm not."

"Someone like you doesn't need encouragement to misbehave, so I'm doing my best to discourage you."

"I try not to smile at you, you might take it the wrong way and be all over me." (Give a fake shudder here.) "No thank you."

"You're obviously a bad boy, so it's a big effort to keep you well behaved."

"I'm afraid you'd take the slightest suggestiveness on my part as an invitation to jump on me, so I try to act like Queen Victoria around you."

**Situation:** You want to get your recalcitrant prospect to make a move.

**Priss:** Does nothing, just bides her time.

**Sow:** Plops herself down on his lap and starts kissing him, placing her hand on the inside of his leg.

**Skillful Flirt:** "I bet you're big on misinterpretation. Like if I was hungry, and invited you along to dinner, just as friends, you'd probably try to take advantage of the situation. Could I trust you to conduct yourself like a gentleman?"

## "You Shouldn't Be Taking Advantage of Me"

If you've done a slick job of seducing your prospect, wait till the point of no return – when sex is inevitable – and tell him that he shouldn't be exploiting you this way:

"Is this what you had in mind this whole time?"

"So I guess this has been your master plan all along, to just sully my purity like this."

"I was pretty much of an innocent until I met you. You've corrupted me."

"One thing I should tell you. I'm a virgin." (If you really want to throw him a curveball, add, "And I intend to stay that way.")

"I have to say, it was really slick the way you got me here."

"How did this happen? It seems I just blinked and all of a sudden we were here."

---

**Situation:** The foreplay is well along. (At this point there is no practical point to flirting, but it's always good to practice.) What do you say?

**Priss:** Nothing, just looks on in trepidation.

**Sow:** "Come on, hurry!"

**Skillful Flirt:** "I guess it doesn't bother you to use me this way."

---

## "I Wouldn't Want to Rob the Cradle with You"

If you're older than your prospect by three or more years, you can make light of this fact by emphasizing it:

"Are you legal yet? Wouldn't I go to jail for statutory rape if I had an affair with you?"

"I'd have an affair with you – but it would feel a little like child molestation to me."

If he's between twenty and twenty-five, ask, "Have you reached puberty yet?"

"Go out and get a little more experience, then I'll have an affair with you."

"I could probably teach you a few tricks." (Every man wants a few more of these in his arsenal.)

"You're so young....it would be embarrassing if any of my friends saw me with you."

"I'm not sure how I'd go about seducing you....I suppose by offering you candy or a chance to play my video games."

"No thanks, I'm not into child pornography or anything like that."

"Isn't there a law against corrupting the morals of a minor or something like that?"

"I don't want to end up on the front page of the newspaper like that teacher who had sex with her student."

> **Situation:** The possibility of an affair between you and a younger man has arisen (he is eager).
>
> **Priss:** Is intrigued but doesn't say anything.
>
> **Sow:** "Are you looking to lose your virginity? Would I have to change your diapers too?"
>
> **Skillful Flirt:** "But I'd feel like….Michael Jackson. Or a Catholic priest with a choir boy."

## "You're a Bad Boy"

If you want to encourage your prospect's naughty side, tell him that that's what he is, with a look in your eye that indicates anything but disapproval. At a certain level, all men like to think of themselves as bad. So even if he acts like a choir boy, tell him:

"I can tell. You're bad. You just give off those vibes."

"I could tell you were dangerous from the moment I first saw you. It's in your eyes."

"I'm a good girl. But sometimes when a good girl meets a bad boy, there's conflict. I don't know who's going to prevail this time."

"Have you always been this naughty?"

"I bet you were a handful in school. Your teachers must have had a hard time with you. You were probably always throwing spitballs and pulling the girls' hair. I bet you were very familiar with the detention room."

If he does anything in the least naughty, slap his hand and remonstrate, "*Bad boy!*"

"I know your type. The minute you meet a girl you fancy, you're sizing her up and wondering, 'Will she or won't she? And if she won't, how can I get her to'?"

"I don't know if I can trust you. Or maybe I don't know if I can trust myself around you."

If you're in the mood, turn the conversation to more physical suasions: "What am I going to do to keep you in line? Am I going to have to tie you up to make sure you don't get into trouble? Will I have to wash your mouth out with soap if you don't stop saying naughty things?"

The concept you want to communicate is that he is naughty, not evil, since every guy, whether saintly or demonic, likes to think himself just a touch naughty.

---

**Situation:** You enter your prospect's apartment.

**Priss:** Doesn't say anything, looks around.

**Sow:** "Jesus, what a dump. You ought to hire a decorator. Or at least get a maid."

**Skillful Flirt:** "So this is where it all takes place? I bet you've had a million girls up here."

---

## "Who Let You Out of Your Cage?"

If your prospect is the type who takes pride in his animalistic qualities, and if he has demonstrated his desire for you, you can stroke his ego and play coy at the same time by commenting on his animalistic tendencies. (This is better than responding with that cliché of flirtation, "You have a one track mind.")

"They should be more careful at night when they're locking up at the zoo."

"Did your parents ever try to domesticate you? Didn't have much success, did they."

"Well I guess you can take the boy out of the jungle but you can't take the jungle out of the boy."

"You remind me of my friend's dog. Every time I go over to her apartment, he starts barking, his tongue hangs out, and he tries to hump my leg. Down boy, down!"

"Now I know why they castrate dogs. We need to put a leash on you."

"It must be mating season for your species, whatever that is."

"It's funny, when I first met you, you seemed like such a normal, well-behaved guy."

Try to sound bemused rather than disgusted or scared as you make these observations.

**Situation:** After a pleasant dinner, your prospect is being very pushy in his attempts to get you into bed. (You've haven't discouraged him so far.)

**Priss:** "I'm just not ready yet."

**Sow:** "Oh well....So how's your endurance?"

**Skillful Flirt:** (with a twinkle in her eye) "You basically turn into a werewolf at night, don't you? It was probably people like you who got that myth started."

# Be Romantic

Flirting is by its nature more about sex than about love, but there's no reason not to throw a little romance into the mix at times. You don't want to overdo it, because men because notoriously skittish when the subject of long term commitment is introduced, but you won't necessarily scare your prospect away by letting him know that you have a serious crush on him. After all, we all know that crushes are temporary things which can disappear overnight, and this may give him motivation to act before it does.

## "I Can't Stop Thinking about You"

If you don't mind communicating to your prospect that you like him, but don't want to use the word "crush" or "love," another way to do it is to confess that you haven't been able to stop thinking about him. No one ever obsesses about someone else unless there's love or hate involved, and if it's the latter, people generally don't admit to it ("I haven't been able to stop thinking about how much I want to kill you.")

If you don't want to be that direct, say, "I don't know why, but you've been on my mind a lot recently." The disingenuous "I don't know why" adds a transparent-on-purpose element.

Or, "You probably assume I think about you a lot. But why would I ever bother to do that?" (This coyly communicates the exact same message.)

Or just stick with the straightforward confession: "There I was in the lecture hall, supposed to be concentrating, but all I could think about was you."

Make it sound involuntary: "I wish I could stop, but I can't. It's a real problem.....I should probably see a psychiatrist."

A more subtle approach is, "I thought of you the other day when I was...." Then give the reason you were reminded (*not* "...when I was masturbating").

The big risk with this approach is that your prospect will take you for granted. You don't want to make this kind of confession to someone who prefers a challenge.

---

**Situation:** A woman sees a guy she fancies for the first time in several days.

**Priss:** Looks the other way, too flustered to be able to think of something to say, then, after being greeted, spasmodically says, "Hi!"

**Sow:** (abruptly walking away from whomever she was talking to) "Hey!!"

**Skillful Flirt:** "There you are, in the flesh. You've been on my mind a lot recently."

---

# "Can You Please Give Me a Reason to Hate You?"

If there is some reason a romance between you and your prospect is verboten, plaintively give voice to the above line. This will communicate several messages at once, all flattering. First, it says that as of now, you like your prey. Second, it implies that you're struggling against your attraction to him – which means you *really* like him. And third, it says that you can't think of a single reason to *dis*like him, which means you think he's perfect (which is how he probably regards himself anyway).

If there aren't any good reasons why a romance between the two of you is wrong, just invent a bogus one. ("I'm seeing someone else at the moment", "I've sworn off men", "I'm trying to concentrate on my career/studies", "I'm sort of engaged, so I really shouldn't be looking at other men.")

This approach is particularly effective because it doesn't immediately sound flirtatious. It is only when the implications sink in that your prey will feel flattered. (A pleasant aftertaste is always more gratifying than a burst of sugar.)

So give voice to your "desire":

"I need to get to know you better so I can see your flaws as well. Whatever they are, you do a good job of keeping them well-hidden."

Or, on a slightly less subtle note:

"I really would appreciate it if you would give me a reason to dislike you."

"You know what I'd like? If you told me you're a [conservative/liberal], so I could really hate you."

> **Situation:** The subject of how you feel about your prospect has arisen.
>
> **Priss:** "You're pretty nice."
>
> **Sow:** "You want me to list your faults? You got a coupla hours?"
>
> **Skillful Flirt:** "There's no way you're as perfect as you seem. Everybody has *some* faults. And I intend to find yours."

## "I'll Always Remember You"

Everyone likes to be remembered, and the thought that they will be a permanent part of someone's memory bank, even when they're old and gray, is very appealing.

Think of the people who have become fixtures on your mental landscape. Aren't there around twenty or thirty people who – welcome or not – keep popping up? Think how flattered they'd be if they knew that they were ensconced there. Use this psychology on your prospect.

Tell him, "I'll always remember you. You're one of the few who will stay with me till my dying day. When I'm ninety and about to kick off, and my life flashes before my eyes, I suspect your face is going to be one of the last ones I see. For better or worse -- probably worse." (This last phrase lightens your speech a touch.)

Point out the obvious: "You should be flattered. There really aren't that many people who stick with me. I actually have a hard time remembering a lot of people I've just met – it's embarrassing, actually."

Continue, as if in stream-of-consciousness mode, "You know, it's strange. I mean, I wonder what it is that makes us remember some people, and forget others. I guess to be memorable a person has to have some sort of emotional impact on you...." The implication is clear.

> **Situation:** Your prospect tells you you're a memorable woman.
>
> **Priss:** "Oh, thanks, I guess."
>
> **Sow:** "A lot of people tell me that -- it's probably because I look a certain way."
>
> **Skillful Flirt:** "You know, it's funny you should mention that, because I was just thinking the other day, you're probably going to be enshrined in my own personal hall of fame -- whether you deserve it or not."

# Banter

Men far prefer to keep their flirting on the level of banter than on serious romance, so give him what he wants – insult him. For many men, banter is their favorite form of relaxation. It's what they do when they're around their friends, it's how they establish that they're regular guys, it's even how they express affection. So if your prospect banters back, don't be insulted, just engage him in a war of words. If the undertone is friendly, it can be fun in and of itself, even if it doesn't lead to romance. But when the banter happens between a man and woman, it often does lead to other entanglements. (When was the last time you watched a movie where a man and woman bantered and it didn't lead to romance?)

## "You'd Better Watch out or I'll Use My Mojo on You"

If there's the slightest hint of tension between you and your prospect, a good way to lighten it is to threaten him with black magic:

"I've never told you this before, but I'm part Creole. As a matter of fact, I'm a direct descendant of Marie Laveau, the famous Louisiana Voodoo Queen. The fact is, I too can cast spells and put hexes on people. And if you don't behave, I'll start sticking pins in the little Johnny doll I have at home. Believe me, you'll feel them. Have you ever felt any unexplained aches or pains before?" Then just shrug your shoulders with a "See?" gesture.

"I'll put a spell on you – I'll have you speaking in tongues."

"I'll even make you my love slave if I want."

If your victim is more the Harry Potter type, explain, "You're only a Muggle, so you wouldn't understand. But I'm a wizard, and I may just change you into a worm."

"Maybe I'll change you into a lap dog…Well, come to think of it, you're already sort of a lap dog."

"I'm an expert at hypnosis. And without you even realizing it, I could hypnotize you into thinking you're in love with me. But I don't want to do that because it'd be a real pain having you follow me around and stuff."

---

**Situation:** Because of unforeseen – but legitimate -- work commitments, your prospect cancels out at the last minute on a romantic dinner you had planned."

**Priss:** "Oh…I'm sorry to hear that."

**Sow:** "*Shit*…You got any cute friends who can come instead?"

**Skillful Flirt:** "You pull this again and I'll use my mojo on you. You won't know what hit you. You'll be skipping out of work in the middle of the day to come meet me."

---

## "You're So in Love with Me It's Pathetic"

This line should never be used if true or you'll turn your prospect into an enemy. Rather, it is to be used in the early stages of a flirtation, when he has demonstrated both an initial interest and a sense of humor. (If he has shown no interest, the following lines will make you sound as if you're making fun of yourself – which is not necessarily a bad thing.)

"You really are pretty far gone…I can tell by that hangdog look you get whenever I'm around."

"…it's pretty obvious from the way your pupils expand whenever you see me."

"…I can see the pulse on the side of your neck start to beat faster whenever you see me."

"…by the goose bumps you seem to get whenever you're around me."

"Aren't you a little embarrassed to be making those puppy dog eyes at me all the time? Frankly, even I find it a little embarrassing."

"Don't worry, you'll get over me eventually."

"Aren't there any other girls you could be interested in? Look at Jane over there, she's a nice girl. Why don't you go bother her instead?"

"You ought to at least make a little effort to hide it."

"Hasn't anyone ever explained to you how it's more effective for a guy to play hard to get?"

Eventually, he will deny it. Just respond, "Please, it's written all over your face whenever you see me."

**Situation:** You run into your prospect at the supermarket.

**Priss:** "Oh hi John."

**Sow:** (peering into his shopping cart) "You actually eat that shit?"

**Skillful Flirt:** "You know, I'd never really appreciated what a stalker was until I met you. No matter which way I turn…"

## "Does this Approach Normally Work for You?"

If you don't want to entirely discourage a man who is trying to pick you up, a good way to continue the pas de deux is to ask if his approach normally works with other girls. This allows you to play hard to get, but in such a playful manner that the message you're communicating is, you're not impossible to get.

Comment, "I guess when you say that you just expect me to fall into bed with you."

"How do you react when you meet a girl who's more of a challenge, like me? Just pack up shop and go on to the next one?"

If his approach is lame, don't be afraid to point this out:

"So, let's see: I 'have the nicest breasts in the place' – what exactly do you expect me to say in reply, 'Hey, thanks, wanna see 'em?' Tell me, has a girl ever responded positively to that statement?"

"You must not have a very high opinion of most women's intelligence if you expect them to fall for a line like that."

Or, "I'd heard that some guys use lines like that, I've just never actually seen one in person before."

"Am I supposed to feel flattered that I'm the eighty-seventh girl to her that line?" When he insists that he hasn't used the line that much, reply, "Well, if you can't remember how many times you've used the line, at least tell me when the last time you used it was?" Add playfully, "Come on, tell the truth."

If he continues to go after you, tell him, "You get an 'A' for persistence. But you get an 'F' for style."

You needn't wait for some guy to use a lame line to unload on him; if you get even a whiff of a hackneyed approach, unload on him.

> **Situation:** Your prospect says, "Did you ever work as a model?"
>
> **Priss:** "No."
>
> **Sow:** "Get lost, creep."
>
> **Skillful Flirt:** "I have to admire your courage for using a line like that."

## Imitate Him

One of the oldest methods of flirting is to ape your prospect in a way that will make him laugh, or at least bring a sheepish grin to his face. Everybody has personal idiosyncrasies which can be mined for effect.

If he walks with a strut, ask him, "Who does this remind you of," then do the same.

If he has certain mannerisms, or postures, or expressions that he overuses, work those into your act. Any overly macho mannerisms of his will seem funny if you imitate them.

Chances are his ego will have expressed itself in some form or another. Lower your voice, say, "I'm [your prospect's name]," and then let loose with the same boast, but exaggerate it. Anything he was later proven wrong on, insist on in a vehement voice.

The idea here is not to rub his face in his sore points, or make fun of his appearance. As long as you only spoof him affectionately for things that he can help, he won't be offended.

You can't pull this act off half-heartedly or the effect will be lost. You must lose yourself in his character.

One caveat: your prospect must have a sense of humor. If he is a narcissistic personality, he may get very touchy about being mocked. If this is the case, not only do you not want to do this, you really want nothing to do with him.

> **Situation:** Your prospect has a tendency to put his hand to his crotch and adjust himself from time to time.
>
> **Priss:** Looks away, embarrassed.
>
> **Sow:** "You pig! Will you stop fondling yourself all the time!?"
>
> **Skillful Flirt:** Takes his hat, places it on her head, asks, "Does this remind you of anyone you know," and imitates the mannerism.

## "Are You Man Enough?"

One challenge no man can resist is being asked by a woman if he's man enough to do some task, especially if that task is relatively easy. This allows him to purchase his machismo very cheaply.

Next time you drop your napkin, give your prospect an arch look and ask, frostily, "Well? Are you man enough to pick that off the ground for me?"

You can use this approach in any situation, and get him to do small favors for you this way:

"I was wondering, are you man enough to put the pilot light back on in my stove?"

"…give me a ride to the drugstore?"

"…lift this suitcase up to the top shelf?"

"…hold this ladder steady while I'm on it?"

If you want to stroke his ego, say afterwards, "Hmm….most of the guys around here don't seem to be able to do that," as if your prospect is a rare find.

The subliminal message you're sending, of course, is, "Are you man enough to satisfy me in bed?" Let your prospect pass enough of these easy tests, and after a while he'll probably feel that he is.

> **Situation:** You want to hang a picture on your wall and need to have a nail hammered in straight. How do you ask your prospect to help you?
>
> **Priss:** "Could I ask you a big favor?"
>
> **Sow:** "Hey, how about making yourself useful for a change."
>
> **Skillful Flirt:** "I was wondering. Are you man enough to…"

# "If You Were a Girl…"

It can be fun to speculate on what type of woman your prospect would have made. For instance, if he's the type of male who likes to complain about women in general, point out, "If you were a woman, you'd probably be the kind of super-feminist who constantly rages about how men are such pigs.

"You'd have been the kind of woman who automatically sides with every woman over every man no matter what the situation. You know how annoying they are."

If he ever loses his temper, say, "You'd have been the kind of woman who's always throwing big hissy fits."

If he's at all critical, say, "As a woman, you'd have been a real nag -- the kind referred to as a shrew."

If he's a ladies' man, say, "You'd probably have been a prostitute. Or who knows, maybe just a stripper -- but one who probably did a little hooking on the side."

If he's not a ladies' man, say, "You'd probably have been an ice queen, or at least one of those women who whenever she has sex figures she's doing the guy a huge favor."

If he's ambitious, say, "You'd have probably been a gold-digger. Maybe even the Black Widow type, if you know what I mean."

If he has an aura of danger about him, say he would have been a femme fatale.

If he dresses in a way that seems at all calculated to get attention, tell him, "If you were a girl, you'd probably be the type who wore low-cut blouses and high-cut skirts all the time."

Basically, you want to just list men's least favorite generic types of women. Who knows, these comments might even improve his personality.

---

**Situation:** Your prospect is a body builder (whom you suspect may have taken steroids).

**Priss:** "You must work out...'

**Sow:** "You know what they say – big muscles, little dick."

**Skillful Flirt:** "If you were a woman, you'd probably get double-D implants."

---

## "Are You Sure You're Hetero?"

This is a tried and true technique which women have used throughout the ages to tease men and perhaps even goad them into action. Just keep in mind, it's unsporting to accuse a man of being gay without being willing to give him the opportunity to prove that he is not.

So, if he demonstrates any tastes that are normally associated with gay men, make hay of it:

"You like the opera? You're the first straight guy I've met who does. Or are you....oh, never mind."

"You go to a manicurist? My experience is that even though metrosexual rhymes with heterosexual, it rarely is."

If he expresses any interest whatsoever in fashion, comment, "Now that I think of it, your male friends are pretty cute, aren't they?"

"Have you ever had a girlfriend? I mean one you've had sex with?"

"I'm with you -- I think men are much more attractive than women. All those hard muscles, the washboard abs, the muscular butts. Mmm."

"What do you do when you see a picture of a naked woman? Throw up?"

"If you ever get the urge to try being with a girl, I might be willing to show you how."

Just don't say these things if you have any actual doubts about his sexuality.

---

**Situation:** Your prospect comments that another guy is good-looking.

**Priss:** "He is."

**Sow:** "He thinks he is, that's for sure."

**Skillful Flirt:** "We should get together sometime and compare notes on which guys we find attractive. It'd be great fun."

---

## "I'm Suffering from Amnesia"

If the conversation has been lagging, pretend to suddenly develop amnesia. This can lead to an amusing, conversation.

Start by asking, "Who am I? Where am I? All of a sudden I don't seem to be able to remember. I must have amnesia."

Then ask, "Who are you, my boyfriend? Have we ever had sex?" If your prospect is playing along, he'll probably respond yes. At this point furrow your brow, and ask, "Was it good?"

Ask, "Am I smart, or dumb?"

"What are my interests?"

"Am I popular? What are my friends like?"

"Am I nice, or nasty?"

"Am I chaste, or loose?"

All of these questions are, of course, opportunities for him to teasingly insult you. Act perturbed when he does so: "Really? Really?" (Anger is out of place since you theoretically don't know who you are and thus have no basis for disagreement.)

Even thought this whole charade is obviously just a fun little game, at the end, say, in mock outrage, "Guess what? I actually didn't have amnesia. That was all just a test to see what you're really like. And you're every bit the cad I suspected."

**Situation:** You're on a date and the conversation has thus far been a little stilted. Your prospect excuses himself to go to the men's room. When he comes back three minutes later, what do you say?"

**Priss:** "Are you okay?"

**Sow:** "Took you long enough."

**Skillful Flirt:** "Excuse me, but I must be having a psychotic episode or something…. all of a sudden I can't remember who I am."

## "I'm a Man-Eater, You Know"

If your prey is the type who enjoys play-acting, and, more importantly, will recognize when you're doing so, pretend to be a Bad Woman. (If he doesn't fully realize you're joking, this approach can cause a man who is just a little too cocky to back off just a touch.)

Tell your prey, "I hope you realize you're dealing with a real man-eater. That's my nickname, by the way – 'Venus Fly Trap'."

Continue, "I take guys like you, chew them up and spit them out all in the course of a day's work."

"After I'm through with a guy, usually all he's good for is the glue factory."

There are strong sexual implications to what you're saying, but not spelling them out renders them somewhat amorphous and therefore harmless. Your prey may ask what you mean, wondering if you are really talking in the sexual terms he hopes you are. Leave it to his imagination: "You know exactly what I'm talking about."

Your prey may reply that he's willing to take you on, or words to that effect. Reply, "Why would you *want* to become a broken man? Anyway, I don't think you're man enough to handle me. You've never been with a woman like me before, trust me."

After he responds, "Try me", or some such juvenilia, say, "I'd better warn you, the last two men I was with both died of heart attacks – Nelson Rockefeller-style. Have you had a checkup recently?"

"You look a little past your prime. Do you have a bottle of Viagra handy?" If this doesn't scare him off, try, "I usually need a tag team of guys to attend to me."

If in fact you are a man-eater, this pose is generally not recommended.

**Situation:** A man makes overtures to you.

**Priss:** Laughs nervously, can't think of anything to say.

**Sow:** "I wouldn't let you near me if you were the last guy on earth."

**Skillful Flirt:** "I should warn you, my favorite sport is taking little boys like you and making mincemeat out of them."

## Play at Being a Femme Fatale

Blanche DuBois may not have gotten a lot of respect, but she was a compelling character, which is why *Streetcar named Desire* was so successful. If you dabble at playing Blanche, you too will get attention, and as long as you make it obvious you're only play-acting, the yuks won't come at your expense.

Don't be afraid to use actual lines from famous characters, just to make sure the point registers. If you're in the mood, vamp it up: "Ah've always depended on the kindness of strangers."

In case the line is not recognized, or even if it is, explain, "My role model has always been Blanche DuBois."

Take a photograph of yourself wearing a black bra, and holding a gun near a (male) friend of yours who is lying on the ground with some ketchup on his forehead (if you can get a friend to pose that way). Put it in a prominent place in your apartment. When your prey comments on it, explain, "That was my husband. He misbehaved." Shrug, "I had a good lawyer."

This time explain, "My role model has always been Sharon Stone in *Basic Instinct*."

If your prey comments on your perfume, reply, "Like it? Cheap perfume is my calling card. I take a bath in it every evening."

If you're wearing décolletage, lean forward and purr, "So what does a man like you want with a woman like me?" Before he can answer, wink and add, "I have a feeling you're going to be disappointed." (This cryptic comment will leave him wondering whether he would be disappointed because he's not going to be able to bed you, or whether he would be if he did.)

Referring to yourself as a "lady" has a certain faded glamour about it. If your prey happens to drop a four letter word, say in shocked tones, "That is not the kind of language a gentleman uses in front of a lady!" Add, "People think that just because I'm a bit frowzy they can speak that way in front of me."

If your prey figures something out about you, respond, "So much for that air of mystery I'd been trying to cultivate."

Camp up your body language: flutter a fan in front of your face, or put the back of your hand to your forehead and announce, at an opportune moment, "I think I'm going to swoon."

Don't be afraid that this act will actually make you seem frowzy – as long as you make it clear that you're just joking around, it will make you seem humorous and bored, two traits which in combination actually render you quite sexy.

---

**Situation:** A woman brings a man into her apartment. What does she say?

**Priss:** "Well, here it is. It's sort of a mess."

**Sow:** "You better show me a good time, or everyone's going to hear about it."

**Skillful Flirt:** "Welcome to my boudoir." (Bats eyes and places her fingertips on her upper chest.)

# Manipulation

Men, by virtue of the fact that they're bigger and stronger, tend to think that they always have the upper hand in a relationship. This just makes them all the more susceptible to manipulation.

No woman has ever done worse for herself because she has known how to bend men to her will. Quite the opposite. Women like Evita Peron and Pamela Digby Churchill Hayward Harriman got where they got because they knew how to manipulate men, how to flatter them into obedience.

Here are a few tactics to sharpen your feminine wiles.

## "My Knight in Shining Armor"

You can kiddingly goad your prospect into becoming just that. Whenever he behaves rudely, just sigh, "Ah, my knight in shining armor."

If you have to cross a puddle, say, "I thought you were the type to lay down his coat in the puddle so I could cross it more easily."

Ask, "If I were being threatened by a dragon, you'd slay him for me, wouldn't you?" This gives him the opportunity to at least say yes and feel noble, or to reply humorously ("If I had a machine gun", or simply "No").

If you need a favor done, no matter how small, ask, "Would you care to rescue a damsel in distress?"

It's better not to let your tone veer into bitter sarcasm ("Well you're a regular Sir Galahad aren't you").

**Situation:** You're hiking through a forest and you come to a five foot ledge which you need help scaling.

**Priss:** (meekly) "Would you mind giving me a hand?"

**Sow:** (angrily) "Well are you going to help me or aren't you?!"

**Skillful Flirt:** (putting back of hand to forehead) "I'm only a helpless female. I need a big strong man to help me."

## Turn Him into an Actual Knight

You can subtly shift the landscape of a relationship by actually turning your prospect into your rescuer in some form or fashion. After all, much of flirting is about emphasizing your femininity and his masculinity.

If you have an unopened jar of honey, pretend you can't open it and ask him if he'd mind. When he opens it, don't say, "Oh, you big strong man." This would probably come across as either sarcasm or play-acting. Just say thank you and look at him as if through new eyes afterward. The mere fact that he has proven his strength this way will set his testosterone levels surging.

If you see your prospect on the street and you are carrying something heavy, ask him if he'd carry it for you ("My shoulders are so tired"). Most guys, even if normally averse to being used as packhorses, will jump at this opportunity to show off their strength.

Perhaps the best way to alter the texture of your relationship is to recruit your prospect to be your bodyguard. Ask him to accompany you through a "dangerous" area because you're afraid of being mugged. (Say this even if you're the one more likely to do the mugging; and the area needn't be dangerous, merely populated.) This will make him feel like a conquering hero, and when you reach your destination safely, well, conquering heroes do want to enjoy the spoils of victory.

> **Situation:** It's late at night, and you run into your prospect.
>
> **Priss:** "Hi!"
>
> **Sow:** "You in the mood?"
>
> **Skillful Flirt:** "Hi! Can I ask you a huge favor? You're probably going to think I'm just being silly, but I'm actually a little afraid of the dark. Would you mind just walking me back to my apartment?"

## "I Wish You Were a Robot"

One way to both flatter your prospect and let him know that his behavior leaves a little to be desired is to give the following speech:

"If only you were a robot. Then I could program you to do the right things, like open my car door first and not burp loudly and pour me more wine when my glass is empty. I'd want my robot to have the same face and body, those are just right. But I'd just program it a bit differently. Every ten minutes it would tell me I'm beautiful, every fifteen minutes it would rub my feet. Every half hour it would ask me if I wanted a drink. And every two minutes it would respond to whatever I'd just said with appreciation for my wit and intelligence.,"

Your prospect may respond (if he doesn't, prompt him), "Wow – that was really clever! Can I get you a drink?" But even if he doesn't, at least you'll have sent the message that he needs to be more considerate, while at the same time conveying that at least physically, he is what you want. Most guys will be flattered by this, since they consider their looks to be their stock in trade, but their boorish behavior to be easily changeable (if it's worth the bother). They assume that since they judge you primarily on your looks, you do the same.

**Situation:** Your prospect fails to hold open a door for you, and it closes in your face.

**Priss:** Says nothing, just opens it herself with a primly disapproving look.

**Sow:** "You fucking asshole! That door almost hit me in the face!"

**Skillful Flirt:** (sighing) "Ah, if only you were a robot...."

## Make Fun of Sexual Harassment Guidelines

Nothing kills lust, desire, and even joy quicker than Antioch-style political correctness guidelines. Antioch was the college famous for having instituted guidelines dictating that any man who wanted to make a pass at a woman had to ask her permission each step of the way, i.e., "May I kiss you", "May I place my hand on the outside of your sweater", "May I unbutton your shirt", etc. Although Antioch was widely mocked at the time, unfortunately, the virus has since spread, and high schoolers across the nation are regularly indoctrinated against "harassment." (Certainly women should not be subjected to real harassment, but as usual, the doctrinaire types gained control of the process, and many of the current guidelines are ridiculous.) Let your prospect know that he won't be brought up on charges if he should act a bit naughty with you.

Say, "You know, I was at a sexual harassment seminar the other day, and they said that if you stare at somebody, it constitutes harassment. I saw you looking at my legs. You know, I may just report you to the authorities. You could spend the rest of your life in jail."

Say these things in a teasing way, to ensure he realizes that you are joking. If you want to vamp it up while saying these things, you can get away with that too.

"Giving a personal gift or calling someone 'honey' is also harassment." Narrow your eyes and give him a suspicious look: "Have you ever done that?"

"And they say that if you've ever had sex while intoxicated, it means you've been raped. *I've been raped!*"

If your prospect has his wits about him, he'll respond, "Oh my god! I've been raped too!" But he probably isn't, so prompt him: "Have *you* ever been raped?" You can both revel in your victimhood.

Add, "Anyway, I'm sure we can both agree that we live in a patriarchal, phallocentric society which oppresses and subjugates women."

The benefit of these jokes is that they will put your prospect at ease, and let him know that you are not the kind of hysterical ninny who swallows the feminist line hook, line, and placard.

---

**Situation:** Your prospect nods at your tight-fitting shirt and says, "Nice shirt."

**Priss:** "Thank you."

**Sow:** "You pig!"

**Skillful Flirt:** (with mock histrionics) "According to Bylaw 422 Code 313 Section 15A of the political correctness guidelines, suggestive comments like that constitute sexual harassment. I think the proper penalty is castration. Do you want it now or later?"

---

## Bottoms Up

The point is made throughout this book that you cannot employ many of the suggested tactics unless your prospect is in a similarly playful mood. It cannot be overemphasized what a positive contribution a drink or two can make towards creating such a mood. This book is not a brief for alcohol in general; its long term debilitating effects have certainly been well documented elsewhere. But in the short term, not only will your prospect become much more uninhibited, *you* will become much more charming and desirable, at least in his eyes. (There's a reason why bars have traditionally been known as pickup spots.)

As a woman, it generally won't be hard for you to get your prospect to drink with you. All men instinctively know that drinking = sex, so chances are he'll be the one to suggest it anyway. But it's not generally considered quite as acceptable for a woman to get sloshed, so you need an excuse. Recite the following:

"I have this theory that drinking makes you dumber, to the tune of about eight IQ points per drink. Anyway, I was thinking that I really ought to have about three or four drinks, you know, just so I can relate to you a little better."

Every now and then, as the evening progresses, make observations like, "Ah, after a couple of drinks, that joke strikes me as much funnier," or, "After three glasses of wine, I'm beginning to see the wisdom of your point of view."

He'll probably respond in kind; you should be able to start a fun, friendly little war. Of course, if he drinks too, which is the point of this routine, his IQ will go down commensurately, keeping the balance of brainpower in your favor.

> **Situation:** Your prospect suggests some beverages.
>
> **Priss:** "Oh no. I have to watch my weight."
>
> **Sow:** "As long as you're buying….You are buying, aren't you?"
>
> **Skillful Flirt:** "You know, I have this theory about how much each drink lowers one's IQ…"

# Provoke Jealousy

There's nothing which will inspire all the ugly male traits: possessiveness, territoriality, the desire to be dominant, and ultimately, sexual desire, than to provoke jealousy. You mustn't do it so unsubtly that your prospect knows he's being played ("I have a lot of guys after me, you know"). You must pretend you're merely a naïve girl who doesn't understand the way men work:

"The people at my gym are so nice. They're always offering to show me how to use the machines." (You needn't specify the sex of those offering to help.)

Or, "I was so worried about being able to finish my paper on Romanian history, but luckily Sam offered to help with my research."

"What do you think about the Drama Club? I met this guy who belongs to it who told me I'd really enjoy it."

At some point your prospect will blurt out, "He just wants to get you in bed," or words to that effect. Breezily reply, "No, it's not like that, we're just friends, that's all." If your prospect asks how you feel about this rival, just shrug and reply, "He's a nice guy," words which, if applied to your prospect himself, would be construed as an insult, but which in this context will sound quite ominous to him.

Use of these lines will shake a lethargic suitor out of his torpor. Just be careful not to be so extreme ("Bill offered to buy me a Maserati the other day") that your prospect will give up in dismay.

> **Situation:** Your prospect seems undecided about whether to ask you out.
>
> **Priss:** Says nothing to him, but asks her best friend if she thinks he likes her.
>
> **Sow:** "Are you gay? You sure never seem to get laid from what I can see."
>
> **Skillful Flirt:** "I'm always getting myself into the worst situations. This guy from [the next town] invited me to a party there and I said I'd go. Going to another party is about the last thing I want to do though."

## Mother Him

Every man likes to be fussed over, so when you get the chance, straighten your prospect's tie, button his buttons, straighten his jacket, and even tie his shoes. Do all of this brusquely, so as not to come across sexual. The required physical contact will establish a certain level of intimacy anyway, which is your real goal.

Scold him the way a mother would, too: "What's wrong with you? You can't go out looking like an unmade bed."

"Do you ever look in a mirror? You'd like what you'd see, if only you'd ever bother to make yourself presentable."

"You're not fourteen anymore."

"The disheveled look is not one I go for. Some people may find it charming, but I don't."

Help him with any sort of grooming. Run your fingers through his hair, as if straightening it out for him. (Chimpanzees engage in this ritual all the time.) Not only will this feel sensual to him, it has a hypnotic effect as well.

You must stop short of putting your hand into his front pocket to make sure it's aligned, but in this mothering context, just about anything else is acceptable. And given that you're not his mother, have no fear, the sensual aspects of what you're doing won't be lost on him.

> **Situation:** Your prospect's collar is up.
>
> **Priss:** Looks at it, conflicted as to whether or not to say something about it.
>
> **Sow:** "Put your collar down you slob."
>
> **Skillful Flirt:** Puts his collar down herself, pats it, then runs her hands along his shoulders as if to straighten his shirt. "There we go – now I don't have to be embarrassed to be seen with you."

## "I Have to Warn You, I'm a Real Prude"

If your prospect seems a little too cowed by you sexually to make a pass, you can relax him by "warning" him that you are in fact a prude – as if you feel you must "defend" yourself against his overwhelming lust.

"The truth is I'm actually a bit of a prude. My friends all make fun of me for it, but I can't help it; that's just the way I am." Even though your prospect will see his hoped for prize receding in the distance, at the same time the prize will seem a little more valuable. (A funny thing happens with men when in the presence of a reluctant female: their performance anxiety evaporates, and is replaced by its opposite, an *eagerness* to perform.)

If you say these things with a twinkle in your eye, your prospect will not be sure whether to take you seriously. So keep him off balance for a while with comments like these:

"In the old days, I would have been one of those vestal virgins."

"By nature, I just seem to be very squeamish about sex. My parents should have named me Prudence or Chastity."

"The few times I've done it, I just didn't enjoy sex that much. I mean, I can see how it could be fun. But somehow the actuality of it always disappoints." All men, rightly or wrongly, think themselves capable of correcting this misimpression and become eager to do so.

Add, "Most guys are just so clumsy.....If the Shakers were still around, I'd probably join up."

"I'm thinking about entering a nunnery."

"It's not that I don't have a sex drive – for the right guy I'd probably go crazy." (Dangle that carrot.) "'But I just don't understand these women who hook up with some guy they just met."

Sheepishly say, "I seem to have a reputation – you've probably heard about this – for being an ice queen. The fact is, I'm not exactly frigid, but I have to admit, I don't spend most of my life exactly on fire, either." (The average guy will immediately think, "But *I* know where to touch.")

If you think you can get away with it, tell him, "I know this is hard to believe, and I'm actually a little embarrassed about it, but the fact is, I'm still a virgin." If he believes you, your prospect will put twice the effort into bedding you, since popping a cherry is a glorious accomplishment in any guy's book.

---

**Situation:** Your prospect asks you back to his place.

**Priss:** "I don't know, I probably shouldn't."

**Sow:** "Sure."

**Skillful Flirt:** "You must be an optimist…"

---

# Downright Unfair Tactics

Men are Pavlovian creatures, and if you press the right buttons, they will start to salivate like the dogs they are. This section will show you how to press those buttons – without seeming to be doing so – and have your prospect eating right out of your hand.

## "That's Supposed to Be an Aphrodisiac"

The list of foods commonly thought to have aphrodisiacal properties includes chocolate, peaches, truffles, oysters, and anything with caffeine in it. (Whether or not they actually have this quality matters not, since the placebo effect can be quite effective, and in matters of love, the power of suggestion is all.) If your prospect ever eats any of these foods, point this out to him.

Then ask, "Well, does it work?"

He'll probably say, "I dunno," or some other witty riposte. Reply, "Well, if it does start to work, could you give me a little warning so I can make my escape?"

He may have the presence of mind to respond, "Yes, it does, as a matter of fact. And I can't be responsible for any of my actions if I have any more." To which you should reply, "Then maybe I should handcuff you to a fence right now, while you're still safe."

Give him an appraising look and say, "You certainly don't strike me as the kind of guy who needs any of those" Add playfully, "Or maybe you are."

"The fact that you're eating an aphrodisiac when you're with me – isn't that a bit presumptuous?"

"You're eating an awful lot – are you sure you can handle that?"

Innocently inquire, "Could I try a bite?" A minute or two later, start to play-act: writhe around as if you're overcome with passion (but a little embarrassed about it at the same time). Say, "Oh my goodness! It's having quite an effect on me. I...I hope you don't take advantage of me in my weakened state."

Chances are he'll play along with your joke, and if the mood is right, the joke could have a very pleasant punchline.

> **Situation:** Your prospect is eating a chocolate bar.
>
> **Priss:** Says nothing.
>
> **Sow:** "Hey, how about some for me?"
>
> **Skillful Flirt:** "Did you know that chocolate is supposed to be an aphrodisiac....?"

## "My Shoulders Are Killing Me....."

Turn your back to your prospect, incline your head forward, and ask, "Would you mind?" He'll know what he is he is supposed to do. Add, by way of explanation, "I had to help my mother paint her bedroom ceiling yesterday, and I'm just so stiff." If he is at all interested, he will be more than happy to knead your shoulders for you.

Don't forget to say lots of appreciative "ooh's" and "aah's" and "That feels so good's." Say, "Oooh, I can never quite reach that spot myself."

Add, "It feels soooo much better when someone else does it for you," a comment sure to put him in mind of the fact that the same is true of sex.

This is not the sort of verbal flirting recommended in the rest of this book, but it is actually more effective. (In a sense, you're dispensing with all the needless verbiage and skipping straight to the physical part.)

One benefit of this approach is that it will tell you what kind of lover your prospect will make. Is he ham-handed and awkward, or is he gentle yet firm? Does he fumble around cluelessly or does he know how to touch?

Every man is instinctively aware that a woman who expresses her gratitude so lavishly for a massage is hardly going to turn around and slap him if he gets fresh. And every man senses that any woman who asks for a massage is probably ready to get physical in other ways too. The nice thing is, you get to send this message in a totally innocent way, since no one associates shoulders with sin.

> **Situation:** Your shoulders actually *are* stiff.
>
> **Priss:** Leans back against the corner or a doorway and presses it into her back, moving back and forth.
>
> **Sow:** "Shit, I wish I hadn't helped my goddamn mother yesterday.....I'd ask you for a massage but you probably suck at it."
>
> **Skillful Flirt:** "I have the worst knot in my shoulder. Do you know anyone around here who's good at massage?"

## "You Must Have Me Mistaken for Somebody Else"

Should your prospect ever make a suggestive comment which implies sexual interest on your part, disclaim any interest by informing him that he must be thinking of somebody else in a way which will spark even more sexual interest on his part:

"You must have me confused with Catherine the Great. You know, the Russian empress who had sex with a horse." This is a myth which is evidently untrue, but which most people have heard, and which brings an interesting image to mind.

"Not me. You must be thinking of the Empress Wu, who had a bed specially constructed so that she could enjoy 33 men at the same time." This will bring an even more interesting image to mind. It might even lead to a discussion of exactly how the bed would have been constructed, and why. (This is what you're subtly trying to encourage.)

The benefits of this approach are twofold: first, appearing an ice queen will make you all the more desirable. And second, by bringing sexual images to mind, you will get your prospect all hot and bothered. This gives you the upper hand when it comes to any type of game you're playing with him, since a man who is sexually stimulated is effectively a dumb man.

Never forget that men are pathetic creatures who, once sexually stimulated, can be led by the nose to do just about anything. You may find the following formula for calculating male intelligence useful: the mere mention of sex will lower his IQ approximately ten points. A glimpse of a naked breast will lower it by 20. An entirely naked female will lower it by around 30. And any man with a full erection is for all practical purposes a drooling retard (assuming he isn't one already).

**Situation:** Your prospect tells you that given the opportunity, he could give you multiple orgasms.

**Priss:** Is too shocked to say anything.

**Sow:** "You? I doubt it."

**Skillful Flirt:** "You must have me confused with someone else – maybe that porn queen who supposedly took on 400 men in a single session….ouch. Gee, I wonder how they managed that."

## Put a Striking Image in His Mind

There are some occasions when you'll be the one who wants to move up the physical agenda. If that is the situation, if your prospect ever scolds you in even the mildest fashion, act miffed and shoot back resentfully, "What are you going to do, spank me?" (People don't normally bring up the subject unless that's a preferred sexual activity.)

Your prospect may reply that he should, or words to that effect. Reply, "If you think you can hold me down, you've got another thing coming. You couldn't if you tried." (How many men can resist this challenge?)

If he still doesn't try anything, add, "You don't have the nerve anyway." This should goad him into action. Keep in mind, you're risking physical indignity this way. But you can probably avoid it, while still putting visions of sugar plums in his head.

Shortly afterward, act mock angry at something he does and turn the tables: "Maybe *I* should spank *you*." (One way or the other, you should be pressing some sort of button.)

Or try, "And how are you going to punish me? Tie me up and tickle me to death?"

Or, "If I were your ship captain, I'd have you keelhauled. Or maybe I'd just whip you."

> **Situation:** Your prospect asks how many lovers you've had.
>
> **Priss:** "Not very many."
>
> **Sow:** "None of your business, jackass. Anyway, I bet it's more than you."
>
> **Skillful Flirt:** "Go ahead and torture me, I'll never talk. I can withstand torture, you know."

## Recite Porn without Seeming to

If you really want to get your prospect all hot and bothered, simply tell him about a "traumatic" event from your past:

"I had the worst doctor's appointment the other day. There I was, at the gynecologist's, and it was bad enough to begin with, I had my feet up in the stirrups for my own doctor, who's a man, and then this other male doctor walked in to ask my doctor a question. I wanted to die. I really have to get a female gynecologist." It's pretty much a guarantee that the only thought running through your prospect's head at that point will be how much he would like to have been in that room at the time, playing doctor with you himself.

If your prospect talks about someone he dislikes, reply, "That's nothing. One time when I was fifteen my friend and I went skinny dipping in this deserted lake near her family's cabin up in Vermont and unbeknownst to us her older brother followed us there and while we were in the water he stole all our clothes. And he wouldn't give them back until......ugh, believe me, this guy was much worse." Your prospect will undoubtedly want to know what you had to do to get your clothes back. You can either say you don't want to talk about it, or, if you're in the mood, embroider. (Either way, you must make it sound as if you hated the experience.)

If your prospect complains about his parents, reply, "That doesn't sound so bad. Once when I was fifteen my mother actually spanked me in front of this boy who used to mow our lawn." (You can't say this is your prospect knows your mother or is about to meet her.) He will undoubtedly ask if she pulled your pants down; when he does, just nod.

If he talks about a brush with the law he had, tell him, "Whatever you do, don't ever get arrested in [neighboring community]. My girlfriend and I got caught smoking pot once when we were teenagers and we got taken down to the stationhouse and they searched us for drugs. Ugh, it was horrible." Your prospect will undoubtedly want to know all the gory details. Tease him all you want.

All men are rapists at heart, and by telling him these stories, you will merely be bringing out your prospect's inner rapist. It's a cheap trick, but it works.

**Situation:** Your prospect tells you about how embarrassed he was when he had to go through the metal detector at the airport four times before he finally realized that he had his car keys in his vest pocket.

**Priss:** That must have been embarrassing.

**Sow:** "You turkey! You must have looked like an idiot!"

**Skillful Flirt:** "Just be glad you weren't on El Al Airlines. One time when I was twenty-two I flew from Tel Aviv to Jerusalem and they actually did complete cavity searches on us...."

# How to Compliment a Sexual Performance

For some reason, neither Emily Post nor Dale Carnegie ever covered this vital area of basic good manners. But no skillful flirt's repertoire would be complete without a few post-coital compliments.

As a woman, you must be very sensitive about this, for men's sexual egos are infinitely more fragile than women's. Tell a man he's stupid, obnoxious, or selfish, and he may still find it in his heart to forgive you (sometimes, depending on the guy, the insult may not even register). But tell him he's a lousy lover, and you will leave a permanent scar.

First off, you can be sure the man will want to be reassured about the size of his organ. If it's small, tell him it's average. If it's average, tell him it's big. And if it's big, tell him it's the biggest you've ever seen.

Of course, the best way to flatter a man is to have an orgasm. If you can't, and you like the guy, just fake it, in time-honored fashion. If your prey needs additional stroking, tell him you didn't know what sex was before you met him. This will make any man feel like a king.

Or, "I don't think I've ever had so many orgasms in one day."

These may be laying it on a bit thick, but, male egos being what they are, most men will be inclined to believe you.

**Situation:** You've just finished up with a man in bed.

**Priss:** "I better go wash up now."

**Sow:** (skeptically) "Have you ever done this before?"

**Skillful Flirt:** "I never knew how much fun sex could be until now. Honestly, with most guys I've found it sort of a chore."

# PART B
## For Men

# First Impressions

We all come to a certain decision within the first five or so seconds of meeting someone new: whether or not we want to sleep with that person. So the initial impression you make is all important. And the first sixty seconds will position you in your prospect's mind in a way which is very hard to change afterwards. So tread very carefully during that crucial time. A good first impression is easy to ruin, but a bad first impression is near impossible to change.

## Stand Perfectly Still

One phenomenon most people are unfamiliar with is that if you remain completely motionless, like a statue, people are drawn to you. (Although this book is about attracting the opposite sex, this actually works on both sexes, though in different ways.)

To understand why, keep in mind that most people are fidgety by nature. They're usually yawning or stretching or shifting or scratching or talking or fiddling. Often they're doing two or more of these things at once. So we feel ourselves drawn to people who can remain perfectly still because they present an impression of serenity, confidence, and focus.

Watch the Animal Channel sometime. In the wild, predators are completely still so as not to attract attention before they pounce and kill. Lions, before they ambush their prey, are a picture of concentration and focus – the only thing they twitch is their tails. This may be part of the reason why a person who is standing stock still commands more respect – because he seems like a predator.

Another message stillness sends is that you are neither neurotic nor insecure. Only someone with peace of mind can stay that way. Try it. You'll be amazed at the way people react to you. And they won't even realize why they're feeling suddenly deferential to you.

**Situation:** Your prospect enters the room. How do you comport yourself?

**Mr. Inhibited:** Looks at her nervously, then when she looks at him, he looks away quickly, turns red, and scratches the back of his neck.

**Hog:** Chews gum with his mouth open while staring at her, drumming his fingers impatiently. When she sees him looking at her, he scratches his armpit and then adjusts his crotch.

**Skillful Flirt:** Stands perfectly still, not a muscle twitching. Waits to feel her eyes on him, then looks at her languidly. The message sent is, "I'm in complete control."

# Don't Stare

If, when your prospect first sees you, you are staring at her, her initial instinct will be to look away, slightly annoyed. It is much better for her to notice you while thinking she hasn't even registered on your radar screen yet.

When you stare at someone, the message you send is that you are attracted to them. And once that message is communicated, the object of your attraction will value you less, since something too readily available is less appealing. That's human nature – we all want what we can't have.

By staring, you're putting yourself in the position of an adoring fan staring at his favorite star. And stars rarely fall for their fans (they prefer other stars)

Another thing that happens is that your prospect doesn't get a chance to admire your looks (if she were so inclined to begin with). When she sees someone who is staring at her, all that really registers is the pair of eyes focused on her; she doesn't get a chance to really take his features in. And her instinct is to turn away. It is only when he is looking away that she can really admire his appearance. This is why you should refuse to look at the object of your desire; she will find herself, without even realizing why, trying to get your attention and possibly even making a fool of herself trying to do so.

**Situation:** You're in a room with a girl whose looks you fancy.

**Mr. Inhibited:** Stares at her, and when she catches him looking at her, looks away quickly.

**Hog:** Stares at her, and when she catches him staring at her, continues to stare, especially at her breasts.

**Skillful Flirt:** Sees her, notices her looks, then quickly looks away before she can catch him peeking. Finds some pretext to walk in front of her while not even acknowledging her existence. She finds herself wanting to attract his attention.

## Opening Lines

The important thing to remember about these is, there's no such thing. In other words, the more anything you say sounds like a *line*, the less chance of success you have with it. Reciting a tired old line like "If I told you that you had a beautiful body, would you hold it against me?" is pretty much the kiss of death. It's akin to a group of construction workers yelling out "Hey – nice tits!" at a woman who walks by. You have pretty much the same chance of success as those guys: none.

The only way you can break the ice with a girl whom you don't know who strikes your fancy is to talk about whatever situation you're in. Anything else – any *line* -- will sound canned, corny, phony, lame, and juvenile. Women don't like lines because is that they know that the line really has nothing to do with them, and that you will just use the exact same line on the next woman who comes along.

There's always something natural-sounding to say instead, since you will always be in *some* situation, and you will always have *some* opinion about it. Are you in an audience, or at a party? Comment on whether it's cold or hot, or boring or exciting, or fun or scary. Talk about someone else there (who is out of earshot). Chances are she has noticed the same thing and is happy that she isn't alone in her opinion. Your comment needn't be brilliant, just apropos.

It's always better to be original and witty and amusing than otherwise, but it's certainly better to be boring than to use a line that sounds like a line.

> **Situation:** You're standing in a line waiting to get tickets behind a woman you find attractive.
>
> **Mr. Inhibited:** Says nothing.
>
> **Hog:** "Hey babe, are you free tonight or will it cost me?"
>
> **Skillful Flirt:** "Is it just me or has this line barely moved in the last ten minutes?" After she responds, he adds, "This concert better be worth it. Have you ever seen them play before?"

## "Your Boyfriend Seems Like Such a Nice Guy"

If you sense that your prospect likes you, but you know that she is dating someone else, the best way to feel her out about your chances is to compliment her boyfriend:

"He sounds like such a nice guy. You're lucky to have him." You can guess from the level of enthusiasm with which she responds whether you have a shot.

"I bet you two last together for a really long time." If she echoes your sentiment, it's time to depart for greener pastures.

If she doesn't, comment, "You two make such a great couple. It would be such a shame if you broke up."

Or, "You two seem really good together. I'd certainly hate to be the guy who got in between the two of you."

If you're actually friendly with her boyfriend, tell her, "I'd go after you in a second. But my problem is that I've met him, and been friendly to him. Usually that just renders me physiologically incapable of ever flirting with a girl." (If you have a conscience, this should be so.) Of course, left hanging in the air will be the possibility that this is not the "usual" situation.

Or say, "This is normally the juncture at which I'd offer a massage, but unfortunately, I both know and like your boyfriend."

It never hurts to bring up a potential sore point: "So, are you guys thinking about marriage? Have you set a date?"

One way to express your interest indirectly is to say, "I hope he appreciates what he's got with you."

Or, more directly, "I wish you'd tell me something to make me hate your boyfriend. Please tell me that he says bad stuff about me behind my back."

**Situation:** Your prospect mentions her boyfriend in passing.

**Mr. Inhibited:** "Oh. I know him."

**Hog:** "I know that guy – he's a dickwad."

**Skillful Flirt:** (mournfully) "You know, it's absolutely killing me – he's such a nice guy I don't feel right even *flirting* with you."

# Let Her Know You're Attracted

Women know from experience that men are very shallow, superficial creatures who will judge them on their looks. Men are in fact so superficial that if you give them a choice of spending time with a sociopathic beauty or a saintly plain woman, most will opt for the former. This is, of course, why women pay so much attention to their appearance. In any case, you must let your prospect know that she has passed this initial test. This section is devoted to showing your prospect that's she is your type.

Don't overdo this. There are times you want to keep your prospect guessing. But you must also keep in mind that a woman is much more likely to be in the mood for love if she feels attractive herself.

The one woman you don't want to use this approach with is the famous beauty, who is constantly told how beautiful she is. She is used to being flattered, considers it somewhat tiresome, and will find you boring if you get in line to do the same.

## "I Want the Name of Your Plastic Surgeon"

No matter how good-looking a woman is, no matter how many times she's heard it, she likes to be reassured about her looks.

So tell her, "Here we are, the Beauty and the Beast."

"You could be a real femme fatale if you were so inclined. It's a good thing you're actually a nice person."

"If I were you, I'd just marry a billionaire and have a couple of children and spend the rest of my life cruising around on my yacht."

Or turn it into a joke. Say, "I'm sort of the same way you are, except on the inside." She'll probably respond, "What?" Reply, "Well, I have inner beauty."

If a third person is present, you can say about your prospect, within earshot, "There's Alison, doing what beautiful girls do." When he asks you what you mean, say, "Looking languid and bored."

You can always flatter her gradually -- piece by piece. Start by saying, "You have the nicest hands. So elegant. Even your fingernails are perfect. Who does them?" Work your way from the extremities inward only gradually; you want to sound like an aesthete, not a pervert.

If you compliment her "inadvertently", it seems more sincere. Stare at your prospect and marvel, "Wow, your face is really a work of art. Your plastic surgeon got everything exactly right -- your nose, your chin, your cheekbones, your jaw line, everything." (You can only give this compliment if you're absolutely sure your prey has *not* had plastic surgery.)

When she replies that she's never had plastic surgery, feign disbelief: "That's all natural? Impossible." She will insist she is telling the truth. Tell her, "Come on, there's no shame in having had plastic surgery. Lots of people have it."

She will continue to deny it.

Eventually relent, "Well, in that case, you're very lucky. I guess the name of your plastic surgeon is God. When He's in the mood He does the best work of all. Of course, sometimes He likes to play jokes, the way he did on me."

"You definitely look like the 'after' shot in a cosmetic surgery advertisement though."

**Situation:** Your prospect says, "I wish I were better-looking." How do you respond?

**Mr. Inhibited:** "You're not bad-looking."

**Hog:** "I wish you were too."

**Skillful Flirt:** "*Puh-lease* – don't you get tired of people telling you how gorgeous you are?"

# Be Sympathetic to the Problems of Beautiful Women

Beautiful women don't deserve sympathy on that basis, but they often think they do, so pretend you feel some.

Say to your prospect, "Guys must hit on you all the time. I mean, you must find it sort of a pain."

Say, "I bet you find it embarrassing when guys try to pick you up right in front of your friends." Saying this allows you to be both complimentary and sympathetic.

Continue, "I've always thought that women like you must eventually end up thinking of all guys as creeps. They probably make fools of themselves in front of you, just do a lot more boasting and showing off than usual. You probably get a very skewed view of humanity."

Ask, "Do you ever find that there are other women who just automatically resent you without even knowing you, just on the basis of the way you look?"

Avoid come-back-to-earth directives like, "Get serious. If the problems of beautiful women are so bad, why do you never hear of women getting plastic surgery to make themselves uglier?"

**Situation:** Your prospect complains about people judging her on just her looks.

**Mr. Inhibited:** "I guess it would be bothersome."

**Hog:** "Believe me, you don't want to be judged on your personality."

**Skillful Flirt:** Says, "You probably find that there are a lot of guys who want to go to bed with you without even getting to know you first," then shakes his head at this inconceivable lack of humanity.

### "You're Better-Looking than Her"

Women, no matter how good-looking, are almost always insecure about their looks. (The average guy thinks he's better-looking than he is, whereas the average woman thinks she's worse-looking.) If you can convince your prospect that you think she's better-looking than a beautiful woman, she will be immensely pleased – and forever grateful.

So, whenever you see a nice-looking woman, be it on the street, in a magazine, or on a movie screen, point out to your prospect that she is more attractive:

"You're way prettier than she is."

"You're far more appealing to me than she is. I mean, she's good-looking, but I'd take you over her any day."

"If I were in a corridor, and there were two doors, and I knew that behind one was her lying on a bed naked, and behind the other was you, I'd open the door with you behind it. You'd probably scream bloody murder and tell me to get out, but…..that's still what I'd choose."

Be prepared to point out *why* you think that your prospect is more pulchritudinous. If she's skinnier, call the other one a "fat potato." If she's fatter, say the other one is "a stick." If her hair color is different, say you prefer brunettes, or whatever your prospect is. Whatever the differences, you prefer your prospect's side of the fence.

You can always fall back on, "You're much more my type."

The ideal situation is if she has a good-looking-but-hated rival. You'll score double points for observing that she's more attractive than that rival (and triple if you can manage to sneak in a nasty jab at that rival, no matter how much you actually desire her too).

**Situation:** You're watching a movie with your prospect and Keira Knightley appears on the screen.

**Mr. Inhibited:** Says nothing.

**Hog:** "Goddamn would I love to pork that."

**Skillful Flirt:** "I hope you don't think she's better-looking than you, because she's not. I definitely prefer having you sitting next to me and her on the screen than the other way around."

# "I Bet You've Developed a Whole Arsenal of Ways to Say No"

One way to tell your prey you find her attractive without actually spelling it out is to let her know you assume she has spent her lifetime fending off unwanted advances:

"You've probably developed a very defensive personality, because experience has taught you that if you're friendly at all, some slob is going to be all over you trying to get amorous."

"It's interesting – your definition of flirting is just to be semi-kiddingly insulting. Most women couldn't get away with that – the guy would just say the heck with you and walk away. But you, you could probably just vomit on a guy and just because of the way you look he'd come back for more."

Say, "I bet you've got steel-plated defenses that even an armor-piercing shell couldn't penetrate. I bet you've got a whole range of responses ranging from the polite to the abrupt, if not downright rude....By the way, which type of rejection did I just get?"

"You've probably never even had the experience of looking at another girl and thinking, 'Gee, I wish I looked like her'." Your prey will almost surely respond to this by protesting vehemently and telling you about some other woman whom she'd love to look like. This is your cue to say, "Are you kidding? You're way better-looking than her!" Even if she doesn't agree with you, she'll take it as a supreme compliment.

> **Situation:** Your prospect tells you about an obnoxious man who was very pushy with her.
>
> **Mr. Inhibited:** "He sounds like a pain."
>
> **Hog:** "He sounds pretty cool!"
>
> **Skillful Flirt:** "You probably have no idea what it's like to be a wallflower. Trust me – a lifetime of being chased is better than a lifetime of being ignored."

## "You Should Be a Playboy Centerfold."

Telling your prospect that she could represent some iconic ideal of beauty will be music to any girl's ears. So tell her she could be:

"…a supermodel."

"…an artist's model."

"…movie star."

A slight variation on this is: "You're another…"

"…Jamie Pressley."

"…Mischa Barton."

"…Uma Thurman."

Try to pick someone to whom she bears at least some likeness.

The resemblance to someone whose looks she is less likely to be familiar with is harder to disprove:

"…the Venus de Milo."

"…that statue of the Little Mermaid in Copenhagen."

"…a painting of Cleopatra I once saw."

"…Helen of Troy."

**Situation:** You're discussing career options for your prospect.

**Mr. Inhibited:** "Have you ever thought about teaching?"

**Hog:** "You could probably go to the Bunny Ranch in Nevada, make some pretty good bucks."

**Skillful Flirt:** "Why not just be a model?"

## "You're the Kind of Girl I Could Never Get"

One way to tentatively explore your chances with your prospect is to express the above sentiment. Given that it is the nature of many females to automatically disagree with you, you are actually subtly manipulating her into telling you that you do have a chance with her. Once she has done that, it's harder for her to then turn you down.

So say, "If I thought I had any chance with you, I'd be all over you."

"Girls like you are just dreams to me. I know someone like you would never go out with someone like me, so I just satisfy myself with my dreams."

"I gave up on you a long time ago."

"Since I can't have you, I guess I'm just going to have to settle. I hope whoever ends up as my girlfriend won't realize that you're the one I really would have preferred."

"I'd never even dare to ask a girl like you out – you're just too perfect. And I'm so far from perfect…"

"You're so flawless you don't even seem human somehow. And we mortals can't go out with goddesses. Don't some cultures believe that if a mortal makes love with an immortal, he burns up afterward?"

"You're so far above me socially that I'd be overreaching."

**Situation:** You're trying to ascertain your chances with a particularly beautiful specimen with whom you have a passing acquaintance.

**Mr. Inhibited:** Gives up without even trying.

**Hog:** Says, "Hey good-looking, I'm single and I'm ready to mingle!" When she gives him a coldly civil reply, he mutters, "Conceited bitch" and stalks off.

**Skillful Flirt:** "To me, you represent an unattainable ideal. Guys like me never get girls like you."

## "Would You Mind Gaining Around Thirty Pounds?"

If you want to let your prospect know that you think she's attractive, one way to do it is to ask her the question above, explaining "It would do a lot for my peace of mind -- that way I wouldn't have to think about you as much."

"Would you mind getting a few scars? You'd do that for me, wouldn't you? It would certainly help me think of you as just a friend – which is what you keep telling me you want me to be."

Continue, "Well, maybe that's a little extreme. How about if you just start wearing really ratty clothes, and maybe stop taking baths?"

"How about if whenever you see me, you have some food between your teeth, and then smile a lot? That would do the trick."

"Or how about a tattoo on your forehead? Something obscene would probably do the trick."

Take the opportunity to make her self-conscious, if you're in the mood:

"Whatever you do, don't wipe those boogers from the corners of your eyes. They're really helping me a lot." (This is a guarantee she'll dab at her eyes.)

Or peer closely at her and say, "I didn't realize you were growing a moustache. That's going to do wonders for my lovesickness!" (Every woman has some fine hairs on her upper lip.)

**Situation:** After you've made overtures, your prospect tells you she just wants to be friends. (Every guy feels he's heard this line a million times.)

**Mr. Inhibited:** "Okay."

**Hog:** "What?! How could I be friends with a woman?"

**Skillful Flirt:** "Okay – but I have to ask you just one favor – would you mind putting a brown paper bag over your head whenever we're together? Don't be insulted – it's for the opposite reason as that joke."

# Be Romantic

Women are hard-wired from millions of years of human evolution to want a man who will love them enough to stick around and help them raise their offspring. This is why women buy so many romance novels. Even if your prospect isn't the type to read them, she is still probably more romantic than you, so do your best to be the guy on the cover of that book.

You may feel a little foolish using some of the tactics suggested in this section. But remember, while ass-kissing in general is easy to recognize when it is being done to someone else, it is hard to recognize when it is being done to us. When you see another guy buying flowers for a girl, you may think it ridiculously sappy. But the girl who gets the flowers almost always reacts by thinking, "Oh, how sweet."

A couple warnings: first, women are so insecure that they are apt to see sarcasm even where none is intended. So if you're going to be romantic, you must radiate sincerity, whether or not you feel it. This sort of acting comes naturally to sociopaths, but the rest of us must learn it.

Secondly, you must be a good judge of your quarry. Don't use these tactics until she has shown some sort of interest in you. There is a fine line between being romantic and being obsessive, and if you cross it, if she doesn't feel the same way about you, that makes you a stalker. But if she does reciprocate, lay it on as thick as you like.


## Deny, Then Admit

If you deny being totally smitten with your prospect, but then sheepishly admit you are, a little, that's tantamount to an admission that you are, a lot.

This is often what women want to hear. Say, "I'm not saying I hear birds sing when you come into the room.....But I do, sorta." Make your admission sheepishly, otherwise you will lose credibility. If you can pull it off, she will be swayed:

"I'm not saying stardust gets in my eyes every time I see you.....but something sure seems to. I don't know what's wrong with me." Your problem will be obvious to your prospect: you're in love with her.

"I'm not saying I'm in love with you, but.....I do have some pretty pathetic symptoms. For instance, if someone else wore those clothes, they'd just be ordinary. But on you....And your voice – probably a lot of other people share that same pitch, but with you it just comes out like music, even when you say the most mundane things."

"You know, I'm not usually one of those sappy guys who gets all moonstruck and dreamy, I'm really not. I just don't know what's gotten into me lately. I'm afraid I may be on some kind of slippery slope." This implication that you might fall even further in love will be hard for her to resist.

"I'm not saying every time I hear a romantic song I think of you, but.... a lot of times, I do seem to."

---

**Situation:** You're telling your prospect how you feel about her.

**Mr. Inhibited:** "I think you're a really nice person."

**Hog:** "I'd really like to do you."

**Skillful Flirt:** "I'm not saying that whenever I see your face the world all of a sudden seems like a better place – but somehow it does seem more appealing."

---

## "I'm Going to Cure Myself"

If your prospect isn't returning your affection, you can make a joke out of it by telling her that you're going to cure yourself of your lovesickness, no matter what it takes.

"You know any good hypnotherapists? I need someone to hypnotize me into believing that I no longer like you."

"I'm thinking seriously about chemical castration, just so you don't look that good to me anymore. Do you know what chemicals I should take?

"I don't like you, I don't like you, I don't like you. They say if you keep repeating your wish, it may come true."

"Where can I find someone to give me the Ludovico Technique? Remember that scene in *A Clockwork Orange* where they feed Alex the drugs that make him feel nauseous and then force him to watch rape scenes while holding his eyes open? I want the same treatment while looking at pictures of you."

**Situation:** Your prospect turns you down.

**Mr. Inhibited:** "Okay."

**Hog:** (even though he's made overtures to her) "What makes you think I wanted to go out with *you* in the first place?"

**Skillful Flirt:** "I'm thinking about wearing one of those electronic dog collars, and every time I see you, I'll just shock myself. You think that'll help me get over you?"

## "I've Been Taking a Lot of Cold Showers Recently"

This chapter is not dissimilar in spirit to the previous one, but the idea here is that you're merely looking for distraction, not an outright cure.

Tell your prospect, "I seem to have a problem: I've been thinking about you way too often, and I've been trying all sorts of things to get you out of my mind. I've become one of those pathetic human beings who runs from one experience to another just to fill up my inner emptiness."

"First I tried transcendental meditation. But that didn't work because my mantra was, "Ommmmm", and that somehow always seemed to turn into "Sharonnnnnn."

"I've been going out and taking hard two mile runs. Then I come straight home and get drunk. Then I turn up the music as loud as I can. And if that doesn't work, I bang my head against the wall for a while. Next I plan to try drugs. There are so many drugs I've never even tried, I have a lot to look forward to."

"I've been going on a lot of roller coaster rides. I actually tried sky-diving the other day. That was good because for the first twenty seconds after I jumped out of the plane, I actually didn't think about you at all."

"This running-around-like-a-chicken-with-its-head-cut-off thing has been sort of fun. You should try it sometime….Oh, that's right, you already do that anyway."

"I've been going to movies, trying to meet new people. But everyone I meet either seems too boring, or just makes me think of you."

"I tried the cold plunge at my health club. And that worked, but for only the few seconds that I was in it, and it's sooo unpleasant."

**Situation:** You see your prospect for the first time in a week.

**Mr. Inhibited:** "Oh hi Sharon."

**Hog:** "Hey. What's your name again?"

**Skillful Flirt:** "You wouldn't believe the things I've been doing to keep my mind off you…"

## "I'm Trying to Be Good – But It's a Losing Battle"

If you want to flatter your prospect and make her feel her powers of attraction are overwhelming, use the above line. Paint a picture of how you're helplessly besotted:

"I'm trying so hard not to like you, not to be attracted to you, but so far I'm not having much success."

"It's sort of like I've got the devil perched on one shoulder and an angel on the other, but the angel has gone deaf."

"I'm struggling valiantly – I really am – but I can feel my self-control just slipping away."

"I want to be a good boy. I really do. But my attraction to you is like a tidal wave and frankly, I'm drowning."

"I'm fighting it, I really am, but I'm afraid the old boy's going down for the count on this one."

"I'm on the ropes here. I just don't have any strength left to fight anymore."

"This whole thing has taken me by surprise. It really has."

**Situation:** You make a slightly suggestive comment to your prospect, and she tells you, "Be good now," in a tone which indicates she's not all that displeased.

**Mr. Inhibited:** "Oh, sorry."

**Hog:** "Be good? I been hearing that crap all my life."

**Skillful Flirt:** "I wish I could look at you and remain cold. I really do. But I'm afraid this is one fight where I'm outmatched."

# "Love is Just a Form of Temporary Insanity, I'll Get Over It"

One way to both let your prospect know how you feel and warn her that those feelings could disappear any minute is to express the above thought. Just act totally disgusted with yourself that you've allowed yourself to fall in love. (This also demonstrates a healthy perspective.)

"I don't know what happened to me. I'm usually much more in control than this."

"This has happened to me a couple of times before, and I've always gotten over it. I'm sure I will this time too."

"One of these days I'll wake up and think, why have I been so silly?"

"I feel I'm in a sort of fugue state. The sooner it disappears, the better."

"I would have thought I was too old for this." (You can say this at any age from twenty-five on up.)

"This is so embarrassing, that at my age I could still get a silly schoolboy crush."

"I can't wait to regain my equilibrium."

"Have you ever had these moments, when rationality just deserts you? When you feel abandoned by common sense? I just know that at any moment I'm going to snap out of it, come to my senses."

Usually, if you're crazy about someone, that person will take you for granted. But if you make it clear that you recognize your craziness as such, and expect it to be temporary, the threat of this loss of esteem may cause your prey to do something rash to preserve it – like go out with you.

**Situation:** Your prospect, who knows you like her, says something about how love is a rare treasure, or some such nonsense.

**Mr. Inhibited:** "Yes."

**Hog:** "That's just a bunch of bullshit. People who say they're in love, they're full of it, all they want is to get laid."

**Skillful Flirt:** "I happen to be in it at the moment, and I'm convinced that some day they're going to diagnose it as a mental illness, just like all the other psychoses. I just hope I get cured soon."

# "You'll Be the One to Break off with Me"

If you want to assure your prospect that she has a future with you, this is the way to do it. Even if you regard her as a one night stand, tell her, "I can't imagine ever getting tired of you. I really can't." This should cause her to feel warm and fuzzy inside.

"If you want to inject a note of realism, say, "Honestly, I get tired of most girls in fairly short order. But I know you well enough by now to know there's nothing about your personality that would drive me up the wall. And honestly, I can't imagine ever getting tired of that body."

"I'm afraid that when this is all over you're going to leave me heartbroken. Oh well, that'll be my problem, not yours."

"Just promise me one thing: when it comes time to dump me, please do it gently. Don't just tell me you're sick of me and never want to see me again."

"I just hope we see each other for a long, long time before you break off with me."

"I can tell you're the kind of girl who's used to breaking hearts. I'm sure I'll just be one in a long line."

All of this will reassure your prospect that you're interested in a real relationship, not just a fling. And it may actually extend the relationship. There *are* people who are so pathetically neurotic and insecure that they feel the need to break things off quickly, before the other person breaks off with them.

> **Situation:** You're discussing the future of your relationship with your prospect.
>
> **Mr. Inhibited:** "I think we should date."
>
> **Hog:** "You and I would make a good-looking couple."
>
> **Skillful Flirt:** "I'm almost reluctant to start a relationship with you because I know you'll end up breaking my heart."

## "Even If I Never Get Any Further with You….."

".....just flirting and spending time with you has been so sweet. It's actually been more fun than a full blown affair with most girls. And even if we never see each other again, I'll always be glad I got to spend this time with you."

This is one of the best tacks to take with your prospect if you *do* want to get further with her. Say, "I can't believe I'm saying this, but you're one of the few women whose company I enjoy so much I like being around you even though we're not having sex." As chauvinistic as this statement sounds, it will be hard for her to get angry about. Continue, "I feel that we could actually just be friends. There's something….I don't know, *sweet* about it. Please don't tell anybody I said this, okay? It would ruin my reputation."

"Even if you were to tell me tomorrow that you never want to speak to me again, I'd be happy for the time I got to spend with you. I wouldn't regret a minute of it."

"Even if I get no further than just kissing your *hand*, I'd still feel that this has been a romantic relationship, even if there's no sex involved. In fact, it's one of the most romantic relationships I've ever had."

"A lot of times with women, if I don't get them into bed, I feel as if I've wasted my time. But I honestly don't feel that way with you at all."

> **Situation:** A woman tells you she's not ready to go to bed with you yet.
>
> **Mr. Inhibited:** "Okay."
>
> **Hog:** "You gotta be *shittin'* me. This is our *second date*."
>
> **Skillful Flirt:** "I'd rather just kiss you than go to bed with any other girl I know."

## "Believe Me, I'm Not Enjoying This"

If you want to convince your prospect that you're really smitten with her, tell her that you are miserable. This only happens to someone who really is lovestruck.

"Believe me, if I could turn this off I would. You think I like being at the mercy of my emotions?"

"If I could click my fingers and just think of you the way I do about any other girl,
I would. God knows I've tried."

"Love is way overrated. It's basically just a huge bother. I can't concentrate on my work, I lose sleep at night, I don't eat as well. It's not much fun."

"I don't like not being in control. And I'm actually used to being in control."

"This is sort of uncharted territory for me." (Don't say "unchartered," a common mistake which makes you sound stupid.)

"I have this ridiculous schoolboy crush on you."

The more you sound as if you hate being in love, the more credible you will sound. Any woman likes the idea that she is making a man feel romantic against his will. This is power of a sort most people rarely get to wield.

**Situation:** You're trying to convince your prospect that you're crazy about her.

**Mr. Inhibited:** "I like you *a lot.*"

**Hog:** "I really, *really* want to fuck you."

**Skillful Flirt:** "I'm like a lovesick cow. It's pathetic. Ugh. The funny thing is, I hate sappy people. Usually when I hear people talk like this, I want to throw up."

## "I Feel as if I'm in a Dream"

Certain evenings – unfortunately, all too rare – have a magical, enchanted quality to them. The conversation is scintillating, your prospect a feast for the eyes, the mood lighthearted, and the weather friendly. (A drink or two always helps.) You can't predict when evenings like this will happen, and you can never seem to recreate them, as hard as you might try. But at least you can appreciate this while they're happening, and you can pass that appreciation along to the one you're sharing it with:

"There's something unreal about this evening. Very pleasant, but unreal."

"Are you sure you didn't slip some LSD in my drink? How about GHB, that date rape drug? You wouldn't have to feed me that, you know." Shrug, "No raping required here."

"It's funny. I feel more alive than usual. But at the same time, I feel as if I'm in a dream. And I don't want it to end. Whatever you do, don't wake me up or I'll be very angry with you."

"I feel as if I'm in a movie somehow. I'm experiencing this, I'm enjoying it, but I also feel as if I'm watching it as well."

"It's too bad that evenings like this one are so rare. I tell you what – let's do this again sometime – the only problem is, this special magic is always impossible to recreate."

"It's funny how on an evening like this all the aches and pains, all the worries, seem to just disappear."

If your prospect obviously feels the same way, suggest, "Maybe we should agree never to see each other again, just so our only memory of the other will be this perfect evening." (Only say this if you're sure she'll disagree.)

The risk you're taking by pointing these things out is that you may lift the spell.

**Situation:** You're enjoying a magical evening with your prospect.

**Mr. Inhibited:** "Wow – this is really fun."

**Hog:** (who would probably not be able to create a magical mood in the first place) "Hey – do I know how to charm a girl or what?"

**Skillful Flirt:** "I feel as if I'm floating on air somehow…Boy, that sounds silly, doesn't it?"

## "I Don't Mean to Cheapen the Word 'Love'….."

If you want to sound romantic to your prospect, explain, "….because love, real love, is something we feel for people we've known for a long time, like our parents or our siblings, but what I feel for you is, I guess, what they call romantic love."

Continue, on in this vein, "You can't compare the love you feel for your family to romantic infatuation. But you can compare romantic infatuations to each other. And as far as they go, this is about as bad as I've ever had it."

"I've felt lust for more girls than I could name. But this all-consuming obsession -- this has only happened to me three times before in my life." (Be prepared to give names.)

"And while what I feel for you is love in the more temporary kind than the love I feel for my family, well, this is definitely a more exciting kind of love."

> **Situation:** Your prospect has brought up the subject of Romeo's suicide over Juliet.
>
> **Mr. Inhibited:** "He really loved her, I guess."
>
> **Hog:** (shaking his head) "That guy must have wanted the booty *real* bad."
>
> **Skillful Flirt:** "I know that feeling" (looking meaningfully at his prospect).

## "I Can't Imagine Ever Getting Tired of You"

If you want to reassure your prospect that you're not like every other boyfriend she's had, and will never take her for granted, use the above line.

Continue, as if you're just being realistic, "It's inevitable. It always happens. People get tired of each other, the bloom just disappears. But…. somehow I just can't imagine that ever happening with you."

"I don't care how many times I might look at you in the cold post-coital light, I'd still be thinking you're the most beautiful thing I've ever laid eyes on."

"Your personality has a lot to do with it. With most women, I can see right from the start what's going to drive me crazy after a little while. With you, there's really nothing."

"The thought of seeing you every single day is just very appealing."

"I think it would take me about a hundred years to get tired of you. And even then, I couldn't see it."

**Situation:** You're telling your prospect about the pattern of your past relationships.

**Mr. Inhibited:** "I've only had two real long term relationships, and both of them broke off with me after a year or so."

**Hog:** "I'm basically a Don Juan. A very successful one, I might add."

**Skillful Flirt:** "To be honest, most of them I've tired of after a few months, but I just can't imagine that happening with you. You're different."

## "Are You a Witch Who's Cast a Spell on Me?"

If you want to emphasize that you find your prospect enchanting, ask her the above question. Then continue, "Because I honestly feel as if I'm under some sort of spell. I'm utterly bewitched by you."

Lighten the mood by adding, "Come to think of it, you do look a little like a witch....I could picture you on a broomstick. Tell me, if I throw a bucket of water on you, will you start screaming, 'I'm melting, I'm melting'?"

"Seriously, though, are you some kind of enchantress?"

"Do you know anybody who's good at lifting spells? Because it's driving me crazy. Can you lift it? How much would you charge?"

"I'm starting to believe in magic. Or maybe voodoo. Do you have a little stick figure of me at home you stick pins in?"

"Can you cast other spells? If you wanted to, could you turn me into a toad? Or shrink me? Say, can I ask a little favor? Would you mind making me a little taller and more muscular?"

**Situation:** You're utterly bewitched by your prospect.

**Mr. Inhibited:** Doesn't say anything, just stares at her with cow eyes.

**Hog:** "You know, I rarely meet girls as good-looking and smart as me, but I have to admit, you do come close."

**Skillful Flirt:** "You seem to have sprinkled pixie dust in my eyes, because whenever I'm around you, I don't seem to be able to think straight." Shakes his head.

## "I Seem to Get a Little Drunk Around You"

Everybody knows, or at least senses, that being in love is a little like being drunk. If the current mood is giddy, it doesn't hurt to note the fact.

"Remember how in high school people would talk about the 'contact high' they'd get from being around people who were stoned? I seem to get that from you."

"Is this what they used to call getting 'high on life'?"

"I'm a little giddy – you're like a champagne that goes down very smoothly. I could become an alcoholic this way, very easily."

"It's not that I get falling down drunk, sometimes. It's more just like being a little tipsy. And the great thing is, you're not bad for my kidneys or liver. I don't get hung over on you. I can still pass a Breathalyzer test. And the drinks are on you."

"You do seem to be a very heady brew. You're the human equivalent of a Long Island Iced Tea."

**Situation:** You're with your prospect, and the mood is upbeat.

**Mr. Inhibited:** "I don't know why, but I do seem to be in a good mood."

**Hog:** "Hey -- do I know how to have a good time or what?!"

**Skillful Flirt:** "Your presence intoxicates me. That's the only explanation I have for my mood."

## "I Don't Want This Moment to End"

If, when you're supposed to part, you keep delaying it with one feeble pretext after another, confess afterwards that you're doing so simply because you can't bear to say good-bye. Any delay thereafter will be a new variation on a theme whose underlying message is that you like her.

"For some reason I always have a hard time leaving you. Let me just look at you one last time."

"I feel sad our date is coming to an end."

"Just one more hug."

"I think your watch is fast. It's only 9:30, not 10PM." When she tells you her watch is accurate, say, "Then let's go on Daylight Savings time a little early."

"Normally at this point, I'm more than ready to leave. But somehow I can't tear myself away."

When she really has to go, say, "I tell you what, when you leave, you can say 'good-bye', but if I don't, it's just because I don't want to say good-bye."

All of this is silly, but what she will take away from it is that you enjoy her company. (It's certainly much better than making it clear you can't wait to get out of there.)

**Situation:** You're at the end of a second date with your prospect, and she tells you it's time for her to turn in.

**Mr. Inhibited:** "Oh, sorry, I didn't mean to keep you up."

**Hog:** "Come on, make it worth my while, willya? I spent *seventy bucks* tonight."

**Skillful Flirt:** "Already? Hmm....I don't know why, I just can't seem to get enough of you."

## If She Compliments You

Tell your prospect, "I've never felt as flattered as I've been by you. It's not that you say more flattering things, it's that the flattery is just worth so much more coming from you. If other people tell me I'm clever, it goes in one ear and out the other. But coming from you, it means much more. I think about it later and savor it. I really do. Anyway, you're going to have to be careful, or I'm going to get a big head."

"If someone else tells me I'm the smartest guy she's ever met, I'm pleased. But it still means more to hear you say 'not bad' after I finish a crossword puzzle."

"If someone else tells me they think I'm the handsomest guy they've ever seen, I'm pleased. But if you tell me, "You take good care of your cuticles," believe it or not, that's worth more to me."

"It means more to me to have you tell me that I did a good job of tying my shoelaces than to have some other woman tell me I'm the sexiest fellow ever."

"And I remember everything you say, whereas with other people I have a tendency to forget."

"Let me put it another way. I'd rather get to make love to you once than to any other woman ten times."

**Situation:** Your prospect tells you, "Nice jacket."

**Mr. Inhibited:** "Thank you."

**Hog:** "I make it look good, don't I?"

**Skillful Flirt:** "You know, it actually means more to me to have you tell me 'nice jacket' than it would for any other woman to tell me I'm the best lover she ever had."

# Banter

If you feel you've come on a bit too heavy, you can always lighten the mood with some banter. This will demonstrate you have a sense of humor (and show you whether she does as well).

Teasing a woman is a roundabout way of showing you like her: everybody knows instinctively that we only joke around with those we like. If you can make her laugh, she'll like you, too. (Think of all the women who say that what initially attracted her to her spouse is that he made her laugh.) There's something about being teased that puts a woman into a more receptive frame of mind.

This is also your opportunity to play bad boy, so enjoy it.

The only caveat here is, you must always make absolutely sure she knows that these teasing insults are in jest. You can do this with an exaggerated tone of voice, a twinkle in your eye, or a wink.

## "I Would Find You Attractive…."

If your prospect is so attractive that she is constantly being told how good-looking she is, take a different tack. Calmly appraise her looks in an insulting way instead. She may find this refreshing, even challenging. Tell her, "Yeah, I could find you attractive……"

"…..if you spent two hours a day on a Stairmaster for the next year."

"…..if you dyed your hair, got some tinted contact lenses, and got your nose fixed."

"….if we were on a desert island and I hadn't seen another woman for a couple months."

"…..if you were about two inches taller and twenty pounds lighter."

"…..if you ever learned how to apply makeup correctly."

"….if it were really, really dark in the room."

Let her know – kiddingly – that she leaves you cold: "I like you – pretty much the way I would a sister."

"When I think of you I think of the geometry class we took together. Or the time we had lunch together in the cafeteria, and that delicious hamburger I had that day. But I don't think of sex."

"You know you're an attractive girl. But not so much as everyone else seems to think. I see you as a six." (Don't say this unless she at least an eight.)

Conclude, "I have nothing against implants, you know."

Remember, these lines can only be used with an absolute knockout who is supremely confident of her looks – a very small minority of women. With a girl unsure about her looks, use the opposite approach (outlined in the section, "Let Her Know You're Attracted").

**Situation:** Your prospect says that someone told her she was the prettiest girl in her class.

**Mr. Inhibited:** "Well you are very pretty."

**Hog:** "I wouldn't kick you outa bed."

**Skillful Flirt:** "I suppose I could find you attractive….if I were wearing tinted beer goggles."

# "I Would Do You if….."

A slightly more risqué variant on the above chapter is to tell your prospect that you could conceive of having sex with her, but only under very special conditions. Once again, if your prospect is a woman used to being drooled over, this will be a line of banter she is probably not used to – and may enjoy for that reason. You should say this with a humorous glint in your eye – but leave her wondering nonetheless. You want to put a sliver of doubt in her mind, enough to make her *want* you to show you want her. So, at an opportune moment, offer:

"Put it this way. Would I like to go to bed with you? Yeah, sure, I guess so. But if there was a good football game on, forget it. You could invite me over to your apartment, ask me into your bedroom, take off all your clothes, spread your legs, and say, 'Come on big boy' and all I'd do is turn on the TV."

"I suppose I could always close my eyes and pretend you were someone else." Then wince and add, "But what if I opened my eyes by accident?! Ugh!"

"You'd have to get me really drunk. And I'm not just talking five or six beers."

"You're the kind of girl, who, if I did her once....I probably wouldn't want to go back for seconds."

"I suppose I could work up a woody over you.....*maybe*."

Say, as if you're delivering the supreme compliment, "If you offered me a thousand dollars to do you, I could do it. I mean, there are *some* women I wouldn't even be *able* to do – even for ten thousand."

---

**Situation:** Your prospect banteringly tells you she knows you're crazy about her. (You are.)

**Mr. Inhibited:** "Well, I don't know if I'd say *crazy*...."

**Hog:** "I'd fuck you, sure."

**Skillful Flirt:** "I guess I'd prefer to do you than to masturbate. I *guess*."

---

## Be a Challenge

Yet another variation on playing-hard-to-get is to present yourself as a bit of a challenge. But this time, the emphasis is on you and your jaded outlook, not on her lack of attractiveness. Once again, this works best with a woman who's used to having men fawn over her.

With such a woman, just compliment her looks indirectly: "Look at you, with those intelligent eyes and va-va-voom body, coolly appraising me and wondering how easy I'm going to be to manipulate. Well I've got news for you, I'm immune. Not gay, just immune. So don't think you can bend me to your will as easily as you do most guys."

"With your looks, you're probably used to guys doing back flips at your command, but I'm not like that. I can tell you're used to getting your way, but sorry, not this time."

"Listen, you're a beautiful woman, I'm sure guys go wild over you, but you're just not my type." If she asks what your type is, just describe something other than her. She'll be intrigued.

"I don't know what it is, I should find you attractive, you're very pretty, but for some reason, you just don't do it for me. Don't get me wrong, I like you as a person, I just don't feel anything romantic."

Or, "I'm confused. You're actually my type, I should be salivating over you, but I don't seem to feel much of anything when I'm around you. I don't know why."

Yet another approach is to say you've sworn off romance: "I've taken a vow of chastity. Seriously, for the next two months, no girls, no dates, no sex. I want to purify myself." Few women will be able to resist this challenge.

"I'm through with letting fleshly desires blind me. A year ago, six months ago even, I would have been all over you. But now, if I feel any untoward urges, I just meditate and my head is clear again. It's a new me."

Add, "I'm trying to steer clear of temptation – which is why I have to ask you to go away. Wait, I have a better idea: stick around, and if I still feel nothing, I'll know I've won."

Any girl will be simultaneously flattered (that you see her as sought after), relaxed (that you're not about to pounce on her), and challenged (that she leaves you cold). Being female, she will undoubtedly want to prove you wrong on that last count. Let her. You might want to put up a little resistance at first, so as not to appear a complete fake. (But why bother?)

**Situation:** A woman flirtatiously calls you a bad boy.

**Mr. Inhibited:** (surprised) "Who? Me?"

**Hog:** "Absofuckinglutely! I'm bad to the bone!"

**Skillful Flirt:** "On the contrary, I'm a very good boy. Watch this." Walks right up to her, puts his face two inches from hers, then backs off and says, "See? I had no desire to kiss you. None whatsoever." If she seems to find this amusing, he then holds his hand two inches from her breast, and says, "See? No desire to touch you either. You leave me absolutely cold."

## Address Her as Royalty

If your prospect puts on any sort of airs, or just carries herself with a particularly upright carriage, address her as royalty. She'll be slightly embarrassed, but tickled at the same time. You may even get her to drop her airs this way. (Don't refer to her as a *princess*, which implies that she is merely spoiled rather than regal and haughty.)

So get down on one knee, incline your head, and say, "Your Highness. May your humble servant be of service?"

Or, "This way please, Your Majesty."

"If you would deign to speak to a commoner such as me....."

"If you're a queen, I guess that makes me....a courtier."

"Are you a good queen, like Mary Queen of Scots, or an evil one, like Queen Elizabeth I?"

If she expresses annoyance of any sort, ask, 'Are you related to that queen in 'Alice in Wonderland'?"

"How often do you have peoples' heads chopped off?"

"If I do something particularly noteworthy, will you knight me?"

"Do you ever disguise yourself as a commoner and go out amongst the people, just to see what it's like?"

If she does something bad, say, "Your subjects would not be impressed if they knew about this."

Ask, "As queen, do you just order people to go to bed with you whenever they strike your fancy? And what happens if they don't satisfy you? The gallows?"

If your prospect says she is tiring of this routine, correct her: "What you're supposed to say is 'We are not amused'."

---

**Situation:** You crack a vulgar joke and your prospect sniffs, "That's not funny."

**Mr. Inhibited:** Gets red-faced and mumbles, "Sorry."

**Hog:** "Will you loosen up for Crissakes, you uptight bitch?"

**Skillful Flirt:** "Please forgive me, Queen Victoria."

---

## "Having a Good Time?"

Ask your prospect this question innocuously sometime. When she politely says yes, reply, "That's good, 'cause I'm not." When she asks why, say, "Well, to tell the truth, you're a little boring." (If you think that she might take you seriously, don't try this.)

Add, "But if even one of us is having a good time, I guess the evening is not a total waste."

Ask, "Can you be, maybe, just a little bit more exciting?"

Continue, "Don't get me wrong, I'm not saying this is unpleasant. Just that I've had better times, that's all." (If your prospect's outrage ever stops seeming merely feigned, desist.)

"Ever notice how rock stars often start out their concerts by asking the crowd if they're having a good time? That's sort of how I see our relationship – I'm a rock star and you're one of my fans. Know what I mean?"

Then say, "Let's get back to the original subject. What can we do to make you more exciting? To start with, you could dress a little more provocatively. You're not a nun -- though you might as well be. And your sense of humor – you ought to read a book of jokes or something, memorize that. And as to your sense of adventurousness, I guess maybe part of the reason the evening lacks sparkle is that I know, just absolutely know, that no matter how hard I try, I won't be getting anywhere with you tonight."

> **Situation:** You're sitting across from your date having a good time.
>
> **Mr. Inhibited:** "How's your food?"
>
> **Hog:** (shaking his head) "I bet your last boyfriend was a real stiff compared to me."
>
> **Skillful Flirt:** "Having a good time? Good – well that's one of us...."

# Imitate Her

Just as females can flirt by imitating you, so you can amuse them lampooning them. It's fun – *and* it gives you the opportunity to explore your feminine side.

If your prospect is a self-conscious sexpot, you can really go to town. Imitate the way she walks in high heels. Bat your eyes, put your hand to your throat, and affect all her dramatic gestures. If she's proud of her bustline, thrust your chest out as you run through you act. If she's wearing a form-fitting top, pull yours on tighter around you. Place a couple of tennis balls strategically in your shirt to make sure she gets the point.

This may even bring out the fag hag in her. (Every fag hag secretly wants to have sex with the feminine, non-threatening men she hangs out with; this time she actually can.)

Any action on her part which is at all transparent is fair game. A side benefit of this, of course, is that it lets her know you see right through her. This should give you both a good laugh, and might encourage her to make fun of you in turn. A mutual mocking session, as long as it's not too acidic, can be fun.

**Situation:** Your prospect is wearing tight, form-revealing pants.

**Mr. Inhibited:** Notices, feels a pang of lust, then feels guilty about this.

**Hog:** "I gotta say, you have one sweet little ass."

**Skillful Flirt:** Growls lustfully, "I swear, those pants look so good on you, I want to… wear my pants the same way." Then he turns around, pulls his pants tight up into his crack (giving himself a wedgie), and asks, "How do I look?"

# "I Can Interpret Dreams"

Telling your prospect that you can tell her what her dreams really mean may lead to an interesting conversation. You needn't be able to actually do so, of course, and anyway, psychology is one of those soft sciences in which it is ultimately impossible to prove most theories right (or wrong). But if you can get her to tell you some of her dreams, it will present a good opportunity to tease.

Get her to tell you at least a couple dreams before you start with your "interpretations." Three of the most common dreams are those of falling, those where you must escape somebody who is chasing you, and those where you find yourself unprepared for some kind of task. (Sex dreams are common too, but your prospect is unlikely to cite these.) It's up to you whether you interpret these in an extremely (and kiddingly) egotistical fashion, or in an insulting fashion.

If you do so egotistically, say that what her falling dream really means is that she is falling in love with you. Her dream of escaping is obviously about trying (in vain) to escape the near total control you wield over her. And her dream of not being prepared is really about how she is worried about not being ready for you.

Or act perturbed by what you're "learning" about her. Tell her that the falling dream is common among extremely manipulative people. The escaping dream is about getting away from the law; tell her that this happens to be a common dream among serial killers. And her dream about not being prepared is common among extremely insecure people.

Be as creative as you like. If she doubts you, tell her that you actually majored in psychology in college, and your senior thesis was about dream interpretation.

**Situation:** Your prospect tells you that she had a dream about you the other night.

**Mr. Inhibited:** "Really?"

**Hog:** "Oh yeah? Did I do you?"

**Skillful Flirt:** "No kidding. What was it?" After she tells him, replies, "That's very interesting in terms of what it says about you. You know, I took a course on dream interpretation in college...."

## "When You're talking to St. Peter at the Pearly Gates...."

"...and he asks you whether you treated people well in life, you're going to have to admit to him, "Well, I was actually sort of mean to Nick." Some might say that invoking the concept of the afterlife in the cause of seduction is sacrilegious. But if it's clear that you're not serious, you can probably get away with it.

"You want to get into heaven, you're going to have to be a little more accommodating to me. That's pretty much what it boils down to."

"You know, I hear that hell's pretty hot. It's not a place you want to spend time. And besides – you already have a nice tan."

"On the other hand, I understand heaven is very nice. Sort of like Club Med, except you never get bored. By the way, if you want a little foretaste of heaven, you could try going to bed with me."

"You should know, getting into heaven is a little like becoming an Eagle Scout: you have to start collecting those merit badges early."

Whatever you do, don't ever try this routine with someone who takes her religion seriously, or your own chances of landing her will be forever damned.

**Situation:** After a necking session, your prey prevents you from going any further.

**Mr. Inhibited:** "I understand."

**Hog:** "Oh come *on*....I'm *really* horny." Pulls her hand to his crotch. "See?"

**Skillful Flirt:** "Have you done your good deed for the day yet? Did you help any little old ladies across the street this morning? No? Well, then it's time you did someone a favor...."

## "You'll Give in Eventually"

If your prospect is playing coy, tell her, "I hope you don't think a simple 'no' is going to stop a force of nature like me."

"No rejection is ever completely final."

"Change your mind yet? You will."

"I have absolutely no doubt that you'll eventually come around."

"You're acting all hoity toity now. But you'll change your tune."

"You know, eventually you'll give in from sheer exhaustion."

"I don't care if I have to wait till you're eighty. I'll get you." (She'll find the thought that you might actually still want her at eighty reassuring, even if she knows you don't really mean it.)

"I'm a very patient guy. *Very* patient."

"I'm warning you, I'm like a badger: I never let go."

"I know you're all pleased with yourself for having gotten the best of me. But don't be too pleased, 'cause I'm going to triumph eventually."

"Your obstinacy is leading to my abstinence, which I don't like."

"Don't you want to say yes, just so that I stop being such a pest?"

> **Situation:** A girl has rejected you. What do you say the next time you see her?
>
> **Mr. Inhibited:** Hi Sally."
>
> **Hog:** "Tell the truth -- you're a dyke, aren't you?"
>
> **Skillful Flirt:** (smiling) "You *think* you've given me the brushoff. But it's not that easy, I assure you."

## "Hey There Little Red Riding Hood…."

If you want to appear less like a big bad wolf, the best way to do it is to jokingly pretend to actually *be* the creature from the fairy tale. (Real wolves pretend to be grandmothers or some such.) If you remember the song from the 1960's, sing it:

"Hey there Little Red Riding Hood, you sure are looking good, you're everything that a big bad wolf could want….."

You can imitate a child molester similarly: "Oh little girl, would you like some candy?" Actually, your prospect probably never suspected you of pederasty, but she will likely enjoy being treated – temporarily – like a little girl. (Who among us doesn't like to feel younger than we are?)

Go on in this vein: "Why don't you come over to my house? I have lots of fun things: Barbie dolls, stuffed animals, video games, even an ice cream machine." When she says no, bitterly shake your head and say, "Things just haven't been good since I was drummed out of the priesthood."

"Why is there such an organization as NAMBLA but no equivalent for heterosexuals? I guess it would be called NAMGLA."

**Situation:** You see your prospect and feel an overwhelming surge of desire for her.

**Mr. Inhibited:** Goes home and masturbates.

**Hog:** "Hey, how about a blow job?"

**Skillful Flirt:** Howls and asks, "Why is it every time I see you I feel like a big bad wolf?"

## "I Bet You'd Be Real Sympathetic if a Guy Were Unable to Perform"

If your prospect ever teases you about being less than macho, shoot back with this line. This will probably provoke outrage, but soldier on:

"I can just imagine your reaction: 'Do me now, you little wimp! What are you, a faggot'?"

After she says she's not like that, reply, "That's what you say, but I've seen what you're like. Any woman who would accuse a guy of being a wimp wouldn't stop there. To actually go to bed with a woman like that......" Give a fake shudder.

Ask, "I'm just curious. What *do* you do when a guy is unable to perform? Beat the crap out of him? Or just post a notice about it on the bulletin board in the girls' dorm?"

Your prospect will protest, but continue anyway, "You know, when you're that way, a guy is even *less* likely to be able to perform. You've got to understand, it's an involuntary muscle. It's hard to get aroused, no matter how beautiful a girl is, if she's a fire-breathing dragon."

Say, with a straight face, as if informing her of something she doesn't know, "You know, no matter how macho they pretend to be, at heart all men are fragile creatures. You've got to learn to handle them with a little more sensitivity."

This should take some of the fire out of the dragon.

**Situation:** Your prospect teasingly accuses you of being a wimp because you were unable to unscrew the lid from a jar. (She proceeds to do so after running some hot water over the lid and tapping it with a knife handle.)

**Mr. Inhibited:** Says nothing, just looks embarrassed.

**Hog:** "Anyone could do that after running hot water."

**Skillful Flirt:** "Remind me never to go to bed with you...."

## "The Only Reason I Talk to You is Because I Feel Sorry for You"

This line is a bit high schoolish, but everybody likes to feel young, and that includes your prospect. (If you're not young and immature, at least you can act that way.) The variations are endless (please bear in mind that each line can only be used if it's clearly not true):

"I only talk to you because I feel sorry for you because you're so ugly."

"....because you don't have any other friends."

"....because you so obviously have a huge unrequited crush on me."

"....because you try so desperately hard to get me to like you."

"....because your sense of humor is so pathetic."

"....because you seem so unhappy."

"....because you're so insecure."

The "charity" variation on this theme also works:

"I consider you my pro bono work."

"I'm practicing to be a social worker with you."

"I'm practicing to be a psychiatrist with you."

"When I was in high school there was this guy who was really handsome and popular, and he used to always act nice to this one girl who was sort of ugly and socially backward. I always admired him for doing that, and ever since I've tried to emulate him, I guess like I am right now."

It cannot be emphasized enough that these lines must only be used if your prospect realizes you're kidding.

**Situation:** Your prospect coyly asks why you want to spend time with her.

> **Mr. Inhibited:** "I don't know, because you're nice, I guess."

> **Hog:** Looks at her breasts and says, "Come on, you know."

> **Skillful Flirt:** "Because I think it's one's duty to reach down and help the less fortunate."

## "You're Lucky to Be with Me"

As long as you're acting like a high school sophomore, tell your prospect how lucky she is to have you. If you're both in a silly mood, this can turn into a fun argument about who's luckier.

"You are the luckiest girl in the entire world." When she asks why, expecting a compliment, reply, "Because you get to spend time with me."

"It's sort of like you've won the lottery."

"I should make you pay me to be with you."

"I know at least twenty girls who would kill you out of pure jealousy if they had any idea you were with me. But don't worry, I'll keep your secret."

"You're like someone who's wandered into King Solomon's mines, but has no idea of the value of gold and diamonds."

"Are you lucky in everything else you do? Do you normally win raffles, make all your stoplights, and find money on the street?"

> **Situation:** Your prospect asks if you want to grab a cup of coffee the next day.
>
> **Mr. Inhibited:** (reflexively) "Sure."
>
> **Hog:** Gives her a long look, then, insinuatingly, "Sure."
>
> **Skillful Flirt:** "You want to go out with me? Get in line." Gives an exaggerated shrug to show he's kidding, and adds, "It's a very, very long line."

## "Do You Get Wet the Minute I Enter the Room?"

This is an approach which is to be used only when the two of you are in the giddiest of moods. Because if this line is not delivered playfully, and if your prospect is not in the right mood herself, you'll come across not only egomaniacal but perverted as well.

So, if you're absolutely sure your prospect has an off-color sense of humor herself, ask:

"How often do you masturbate while thinking about me? Do you have to masturbate after every time you see me?"

"Do you ever go a whole minute without thinking about me?"

"You should probably see a psychiatrist about your obsession with me."

"Just looking at me seems to be foreplay for you."

"Sexually speaking, you sort of remind me of a vacuum cleaner."

"I'm afraid you'd be a little too much woman for me. I'm not sure I could handle you. Or more to the point, live up to all your fantasies about me. You make me feel...gay"

"You sort of come across like a motorcycle mama, one of those babes who used to ride with the Hell's Angels."

**Situation:** You're describing your prospect's attitude towards you.

**Mr. Inhibited:** "I think you and I get along well."

**Hog:** (shrugging) "All the bitches like me."

**Skillful Flirt:** "Your lust for me is actually a little intimidating. I doubt I could satisfy it."

## "If I Put My Mind to Seducing You, You'd Be Absolutely Powerless to Resist"

Playfully insist to your prospect that if you wanted to, you could seduce her with the greatest of ease. She will of course deny it, but keep insisting. (Make very sure she knows you're joking; if she thinks you're serious it will give her incentive to resist.) The idea is to make fun of yourself and give her an opportunity to laugh at your mockery of ridiculously overblown self-confidence.

"If I actually wanted to get you in bed, it'd be like taking candy from a baby."

"If I had the least bit of desire for you, you wouldn't stand a chance."

"I'd be sending all sorts of subliminal messages that would have you practically raping me. You'd be putty in my hands."

"Believe me, I'd be a puppeteer and you'd be the marionette. You'd have about as much free will as that guy in 'The Manchurian Candidate'."

"I'd exert total mind control over you. You'll be my absolute love slave."

"Everybody would be asking, 'Hey, what's that wrapped around your little finger?' and I'd have to say 'Oh, it's just Susan'."

**Situation:** Your prospect teasingly says that you need to work on your seduction skills.

**Mr. Inhibited:** "I know."

**Hog:** "Hey, I get *plenty* of pussy. Any time I want."

**Skillful Flirt:** "Believe me, if I had the slightest interest in seducing you, you'd be helpless before the onslaught. You'd find yourself doing all sorts of things around me you couldn't even explain."

# "If You Touch Me One More Time….."

If your prospect brushes up against you accidentally – or not so accidentally – you can use that as an excuse to threaten: "I'm warning you: if you touch me one more time like that I can't be responsible for my behavior. I might just misinterpret it and forget that I'm supposed to be a gentleman."

"Consider this your last warning. You brush up against me again and I may just try to kiss you. Or worse."

"One more touch like that and I'm going to forget all the lessons my mother taught me about being well-behaved."

"If you lean against me like that again, I may just…..ask you out."

"You *do* know what message you're sending me by touching your hand to my forearm like that, don't you? '*Please ravish me*'."

One benefit to this approach is that it leaves no doubt about her complicity should she brush up against you again.

**Situation:** Your prospect looks at something you're reading over your shoulder, touching the back of your arm with her breast.

**Mr. Inhibited:** Jerks away as if he's been scalded, afraid he might be doing something wrong.

**Hog:** Pushes his arm backwards a touch, in order to get a better "feel" with the back of his arm.

**Skillful Flirt:** "Consider this your last warning. If you lean against me like that one more time I'll consider it an invitation to kiss you."

## "You'd Have Been the Kind of Guy Who….."

One fun game to play with your prospect is to posit what type of guy she would have been had she been born male. There are basically two tacks to take here: either that she would have been obnoxiously male, or that she would have been completely prissy and denatured. So if she shows the slightest tendencies in either direction, make light of it:

"It's a good thing you were born a girl, 'cause if you'd been a guy, you'd have been one of those fraternity guys who are proud of their beer bellies and who make a pass at every girl they see."

"If you'd just inherited a Y chromosome instead of that other X, you'd have probably turned into a real bully, the kind of guy who's always disparaging other guys' masculinity, accusing them of being gay and so on."

Alternatively, "It's a good thing you're a girl, 'cause if you'd been a guy, you'd have been a complete wimp – the type who always gets picked on by other guys."

"…one of those guys who's a social outcast because he's so geeky."

"…ended up like that guy in the movie, the 40-year-old virgin."

"…a transvestite prostitute."

"…A peeping Tom."

"…a child molester."

Whichever direction you go in, you should get an outraged response, which is half the purpose of flirting.

**Situation:** Your prospect mentions that she's glad she's a girl.

**Mr. Inhibited:** "I'm glad you are too."

**Hog:** "You're kidding, right? I know you're not supposed to say it, but let's face it, women are basically meant to be servants."

**Skillful Flirt:** We're *all* lucky you're a girl -- 'cause if you'd been a guy, you probably would have been a rapist and murderer. But maybe I'm being too harsh. Maybe you would have just been a carjacker or bank robber."

# "Shopping for a Boyfriend?"

Unattached women often insist that they're not looking for a boyfriend, and that they simply don't have time for one. This is of course ridiculous: we're all human and a human's purpose in life is to procreate. (And, by the way, the more a woman insists she's not in the market, the less true it is.)

It's up to you to call her on this. When she tells you she's not looking for a beau, tell her, "I don't buy that for a second. You're probably sizing me up right now, thinking, 'I wonder how much money he makes....Hmm, I wonder if he's any good in bed.' Well, I can tell you right now, I'm poor, but I'm a lot of fun in bed."

"Tell me, when you go shopping, what's tops on your list? Looks or personality? Well, with you I'm guessing it's probably money. Sorry, guess I don't measure up."

"It's actually pretty obvious. You might as well just hang a sign around your neck saying, 'In the market'."

"It's almost as if you have a tattoo on your forehead reading, 'Available'."

Expect all of these accusations to be met with denials.

**Situation:** Your prospect perks up when someone mentions a party where some eligible men will be present.

**Mr. Inhibited:** (hurt) Says nothing.

**Hog:** "What do you need them for? I guarantee you, I'll give you all you can handle."

**Skillful Flirt:** "Keep those eyes peeled, Mr. Right might be just around the corner. Or who knows, he could be standing right in front of you and you might not even know it."

## "You Need Sex Really Badly, Don't You?"

One of the easiest ways to banter is to accuse your prospect of being sexually frustrated. She will of course laughingly deny it, but insist that you understand her better than she does herself:

"Your body language really gives you away. I read a book on body language once, and you have all the classic signs of sexual frustration."

"I can tell by the way you keep crossing and uncrossing your legs.....by the way you put that pencil in your mouth."

"Chewing on ice is supposed to mean that you're trying to repress your sexuality."

"That drumbeat you play with your hands on your thighs really says it all."

"Letting your mouth hang open like that is supposed to be a sign of invitation."

"...The way you keep fiddling with your hair."

"...The way you run your fingers over the tabletop."

"If you just had one orgasm you'd find it's impossible to be in the kind of bad mood you always seem to be in."

The second part of this routine is when you tell her what the solution to her problem is:

"You'd be in a much better mood if you got some....You just need to find someone who knows what he's doing."

"Maybe you should invest in some toys…" (It's pretty clear what type of toys you are referring to.)

**Situation:** Your prospect keeps running her fingers along the tines of her fork.

**Mr. Inhibited:** Doesn't notice because he's too worried about the impression he's making.

**Hog:** Doesn't notice because he's ogling her breasts.

**Skillful Flirt:** "You do know what message you're sending with your fingers, don't you?"

# Advertise

As any good salesperson knows, your prospect cares little about your concerns, she cares only about what you can do for her. And, what you can do for her as a lover is, well, be a good lover. The problem is, how do you communicate that? You can't come out and say, "Baby, I'll give you multiple orgasms," or you'll sound like a pervert. But there are ways to say that without being quite so direct. This section contains a number of ways to do so. It also shows you how to portray yourself as secure, playful, kind, and humorous – no matter how far each of these things is from the truth.

The key here is subtlety: you're only allowed to boast in an indirect way. Nobody, including your prospect, likes a braggart. This is why you must employ these roundabout ways that doesn't come across as boasting to let her know what good company you would be.

## "I'm So Good in Bed Women Often Expire of Pleasure"

Most people are aware that every joke contains a grain of truth, so this is a good joke to make to your prospect. Be sure to make it obvious you're saying so in a humorous spirit:

"I used to have brief affairs, but even after that, the women would get so addicted to my brand of sex that when I wanted to call it off they would offer to pay me for a while. Hey, I wasn't proud to be a gigolo, but it's a living. Eventually I felt guilty about being like a drug pusher who would get school kids addicted and then make them pay for the dope, so I stopped."

"You ever hear of spontaneous combustion? I can tell you for a fact it's real, 'cause two different women I was with actually just burned up right in front of my eyes – all that was left were some ashes. That's why I only use my B game these days."

"I basically ruin women. Once they've been with me, other guys are pretty much useless to them."

"It's a real pain. I have to change my phone number at least once a year."

Your prospect of course won't believe your tall tales. But the mere fact that you've brought up the subject and are joking about it shows that you have some self-confidence in that regard, self-confidence which is probably at least somewhat justified.

**Situation:** A girl teasingly says she doubts you'd be good in bed.

**Mr. Inhibited:** "No? Why do you say that?"

**Hog:** "Bullshit! I'll make you come so many times you won't be able to tell up from down!"

**Skillful Flirt:** (with a glint in his eye) "I've actually given several women who weren't used to having so much pleasure minor heart attacks. Why do you think I had to learn CPR?"

## "Sex Is Far Better for Women than for Men"

For a man, any woman, as long as she is attractive and willing, is good in bed. For a woman, men provide a much wider range of experiences – mostly because of the difference in knowledge (and desire to please) among men. If you happen to catch your prospect in a bantering mood, and she is not prudish, using this title of this chapter is a great way for you to advertise your sexual prowess. Yet it will just sound as if you're just making a generalized observation, not a personal boast.

So if the subject of sex comes up, comment offhandedly, "It's always been my impression that sex is much better for women than for men."

If she contradicts you, continue, "Don't get me wrong. There's nothing I like more. But I never go out of my mind during sex, it never makes me act crazy the way some women do."

"Plus women can have all those orgasms. Me, I have one and I'm done for another half hour." (This advertises your potency.)

"Hey, it's not that I'm so good in bed, but women do seem to just lose themselves in sex." (This proves that you *are* good in bed.)

At some point your prospect will shoot back that most guys certainly seem to enjoy sex. Reply, in a reasonable tone of voice, "Yes, but I never go into delirium -- I always remember who I am and where I am. You never hear about a *guy* who's a screamer, do you?"

Add, "When that couple on the other side of the wall of your motel room is making a racket during sex, who's usually doing all the shrieking?"

Your prey may reply that such women are merely faking it for the benefit of the guy. Counter this with, "The proof of what I'm saying is that sex can actually change a woman's personality. You can take the bitchiest woman in the world, who beforehand will be doing nothing but carping and complaining and insulting you, and afterwards even she will be in a good mood."

All of this talk should pique your prospect's curiosity. If it doesn't, you can be pretty sure that she's not interested in you. But at least you won't have to waste any more time this way.

---

**Situation:** Your prospect expresses the thought that men are usually interested in only one thing.

**Mr. Inhibited:** (blushing) "Well, that's not always true."

**Hog:** (nodding to confirm this thought) "Well duh! What else would you want a woman for? Far as I'm concerned, a good girl is one who gives you a blow job and then just disappears."

**Skillful Flirt:** "You're right, it always seems to be the men doing the chasing, but what's strange is that women always seem to enjoy the sex itself so much more...."

---

# "I'm Getting a Little Too Old for Sex"

We always feel old long before we actually get that way, because no matter what age we are, we're always the oldest that we've ever been. So whatever age you are (from twenty-five on up), if you're older than your prospect, tell her that you're too old for sex. If any of these lines were true, you obviously wouldn't be joking about it as it would be a sore point:

"You know, sex is just a fond memory for me now."

"I might be able to do it, but I'd probably be risking a heart attack."

"The chances of my being able to perform are only about one in ten these days. But I'm too proud to use Viagra."

"Now that I'm thirty, it's getting so I'm not even sure when I've had an orgasm anymore."

"Sex? I think I remember how to do it…but it's been so long…though they say it's like riding a bicycle."

"We could have sex. But I have to warn you, I'm not as limber as I used to be. Basically, you'd have to be on top and do all the work."

Your prospect should realize that you wouldn't be saying any of these things if they were actually true.

Or you can just boast: "I'm getting pretty old – I'm down to three or four times a night."

**Situation:** You're a forty-year-old man angling for an affair with a twenty six-year-old woman. What do you tell her?

**Mr. Inhibited:** "I guess this must feel a little May-December-ish to you."

**Hog:** "I'm every bit the man I ever was. And that's saying a lot."

**Skillful Flirt:** "You really ought to try an affair with an older man sometime – you know, just to see how little you have to look forward to."

# "I'm Straight, But Just Barely"

Ben Franklin once famously said that only two things are certain in life, death and taxes. Actually, there's a third thing. At some point in your life, someone will tease you about being gay – whether you are or not. Rather than react like a scalded cat, calmly reply with the above line.

Add, "I'm straight, but I seem to have a lot of the characteristics of gay guys. I love Rodgers and Hammerstein tunes, I like shopping, I enjoy the opera, and I pay attention to my clothes. The really scary thing is, I don't like any of the regular guy things – football, beer, and cars. It worries me."

"Most of my guy friends are really good-looking. It's not like I purposely chose them for that, it just sort of ended up that way....I don't know."

"I *think* I'm straight. I mean, I've never had sex with a guy. At least not yet."

"I think it would take only a little push for me to start playing for the other team."

"If you don't go out with me, I may just go over to the other side."

"I'm straight – well, maybe I bend just a little to the left. I prefer women with small breasts and not too large hips – does that make me sort of half a fag?"

"Sometimes I wonder if I'm one of those guys who's in denial."

"I'm not a homo – but maybe you could call me a heteromo."

"Listen, I wish I were one of those guys who never worries about taking a bath or using deodorant or making sure his belt and shoes match, but I'm not."

"I wish I were gay, actually.....My sex life would certainly be better. When I really think about it, I *hate* being straight. Women are just such a pain – you have to romance them, spend money on them, pretend you like them, pretend you respect them. Then, maybe, *just maybe*, they'll go to bed with you. You don't have to do any of that with guys. Think about it – if you're gay, it's the equivalent of being able to sleep with every beautiful girl you see – pretty much just by snapping your fingers."

The basic message you're communicating here is that you're secure enough to strike a pose that most guys would be too insecure to strike – which makes you a good companion.

**Situation:** Your prospect teasingly asks you if you're gay.

**Mr. Inhibited:** "No, I'm not! Really!"

**Hog:** "Are you shitting me?! I hate faggots! My buddies and I beat the shit out of them every chance we get."

**Skillful Flirt:** (with a perplexed look) "Honestly? I haven't made up my mind yet."

# When She Tells You You're Trouble…

Don't deny it. Instead reply, "With a Capital T." Denying it makes you sound as if you have something to hide. But agreeing with a wink makes you look as if you understand her position completely, in fact agree with it, but that it really isn't something she should worry about. Your statement will also exude a certain "You ain't seen nothing yet" spirit, which most women find amusing, if not downright appealing.

The wonderful thing about the "with a capital" reply is that it can be used in any situation where you are accused of something naughty.

If she says, "You're a bad boy, simply reply, "With a capital B."

Even if you're accused of something you don't particularly want to plead guilty to, it's better to roll with the punches. If she calls you stupid, reply, "With a capital S." By agreeing with her this way, it actually makes you look less stupid, since you've acknowledged whatever error you've just made, as well as made it clear that intelligence is not a sensitive topic for you.

Another advantage to this formulation is that it doesn't require much thought or creativity, you only need know how to spell. (If she says, "You're a real curmudgeon," and you reply, "With a capital K,' she won't be impressed.) You just can't keep using this "with a capital" line over and over with the same prospect.

In any case, everyone knows that Bad Boys who are Trouble are lots of Fun, so this line of talk should keep your prospect intrigued.

> **Situation:** Your prospect flirtatiously says, "I can tell, you're trouble."
>
> **Mr. Inhibited:** "I don't think so. Anyway, I try not to be."
>
> **Hog:** "You're pretty much a pain in the ass yourself."
>
> **Skillful Flirt:** "Oh you don't know the half of it…"

## "A Little Advertisement"

All men are guilty of slipping up and boasting from time to time. Half the time the boast seems to be out of our mouths before we even realize it, like an unintentional burp. (And they're usually about as welcome to our audience.)

However, there is a way to recover, unlike with a burp. Just say, "That was a little advertisement for myself, by the way – in case you couldn't tell."

She'll probably reply, "Oh, I could tell," or something to that effect. Reply, "I had faith in you. I knew you'd be able to see right through me."

Add, "I guess I'm not above doing a little advertising from time to time. You know what they say – a business has got to advertise. You can't just rely on word of mouth."

Say, "Some people complain that there's too much advertising on this show," as you tap yourself on the chest. "But I see advertising as a necessary evil. After all, if I hadn't blurted that out, how would you have ever known I was a good masseur? And that is something you absolutely needed to know."

Add, "It's funny, whenever I boast like that, right afterwards I always want to wince, but the boast have escaped before I can do anything about it."

"I'm very discreet – I never kiss and tell….."

"My last three girlfriends said they didn't know what sex was before they met me…."

**Situation:** Your prospect mentions that her cousin, who's really smart, got a 760 on his math SAT; before you know it you've blurted out that you got a 780.

> **Mr. Inhibited:** "But a 760 is still really good."

> **Hog:** "So as smart as he is, that makes me even smarter."

> **Skillful Flirt:** "I must want really badly to impress you the way I just blurt stuff like that out. Honestly, I tried to squelch it but it was already out of my mouth – my boasts are just too quick for me."

## "Oh, I'm Soooo Good-Looking"

If, during the course of flirting, your prospect tells you you're good-looking, disagree. She'll find this charming. People always prefer others who aren't too taken with themselves, so whether or not you are, at least pretend not to be.

One way to do this is with sarcasm: "Oh, yeah, I'm *soooo* cute. Every time I look in the mirror I give myself a hard on."

Or, "That's why I never get laid. I only want to make love to girls as good-looking as me, and I can never find anyone like that."

"You should see my apartment -- nothing but mirrors. For me, it's heaven."

Or you can just try simple disagreement:

"Believe me, I don't stop traffic."

If you're over thirty, reply, "Maybe ten years ago. Certainly not now. But thank

you anyway."

"Do you normally wear glasses?"

Or ask, "Are you drunk or something? You seem to be wearing some pretty thick beer goggles right now."

**Situation:** Your prospect tells you she thinks you're handsome.

**Mr. Inhibited:** "Really? Thanks."

**Hog:** "You got *that* right – I am *damned* good-looking."

**Skillful Flirt:** (pointing to his one flaw) "This bulbous nose of mine is a regular work of art, isn't it?"

# Manipulation

You've probably heard the expression, "All's fair in love and war." This basically translates as, "Love is war," given which, you don't want to come to the battlefield unarmed. After all, women manipulate us all the time (refer to the first half of this book). You must respond in kind. This section will provide you some effective weapons.

The fact is, people try to manipulate each other all the time. The only difference is that some are skillful at it, some not. And the degree of skill usually depends on how subtle one is in one's efforts: games are effective only to the extent that your prospect doesn't realize she's being played. Here are some ways to manipulate your prospect into a more receptive frame of mind.

## Vamp It Up

Many men feel that if they budge from their usual monotone their masculinity will somehow be compromised. (This is the same reason why so many men refuse to speak French with the proper accent – it makes them feel feminine.) This is, of course, silly. If you make your voice mellifluous and expressive, it only means that you're comfortable enough with your masculinity to be expressive.

Flirting is all about being playful, and being playful means taking on different roles – which means breaking out of your usual monotonic delivery. The fact is, it's awfully hard to be lightheartedly playful if all you ever do is speak in the same harsh bark.

You can also invest your words with more meaning if you deliver them with a tremulous pathos. Try the following in the privacy of your own room. First, say "You are so beautiful" in a robotic monotone. Then say it again, drawing out the word "so" and the first syllable of "beautiful," and vary your pitch. Didn't the second rendition sound a bit more heartfelt?

Another benefit is that you actually sound more intelligent, when you let your voice range. (You're not necessarily either, but at least you *sound* smarter and more sincere.) You also sound a bit less like either a young guy trying to prove his masculinity, or a gruff older guy – and most women know from experience that both types tend to be poor company.

If your worst fears are realized and your prospect does begin to wonder if you're gay, just think what a pleasant surprise it will be when she finds you're not. (The average woman's ideal mate combines the sensibilities of a gay man with the ardency of a hetero anyway.)

## "I Don't Know Whom I Have More of a Crush on, You or Him"

Tell your prospect about how much you admire some friend of yours. This will make you seem less narcissistic (narcissists always hate to give others credit) and more secure (insecure guys always worry about appearing gay). It will also make you seem generous with your praise – in other words, an all-around decent guy.

After you have gone on in this vein for a while, quote the headline of this chapter. This accomplishes several things at once. It shows you capable of self-deprecation. It makes a joke out of your "infatuation." It makes you seem less threatening. It establishes that you do in fact have a crush on your prospect. And it establishes your heterosexuality (no actual gay guy would phrase it that way).

Ask with mock concern, "Seriously, do you think this makes me half a homo?" (If you were actually concerned about this, you would never have gone on about your friend in the first place.)

**Situation:** You've just raved about what a great basketball player a friend of yours is, and you're feeling a touch sheepish about your unabashed enthusiasm.

**Stiff:** "....But I guess there are other good basketball players out there too."

**Hog:** "....Anyway, it's too bad he's such an asshole."

**Skillful Flirt:** ""I guess this is what they call a 'man crush'."

## "We're Like Fred and Ginger"

Whenever you and your prospect are in a new situation, invoke the names of a famous couple associated with those circumstances. So, when the two of you go dancing, say, jocularly, "We're like Fred and Ginger." It's silly, but somewhere in the back of her mind she'll feel just a tiny bit more glamorous because of it.

If the two of you have even a mild rooting interest in opposing teams, point out, "We're like Romeo and Juliet. You're a Knick and I'm a Celtic"

If you come from different cultures, say, "We're like John Smith and Pocohontas."

If she is divorced, say, "We're like Prince Edward and Wallis Simpson."

If either of you is married, say, "We're like JFK and Marilyn Monroe."

If anyone calls you a good-looking couple, say, "We're another Brangelina."

She should be amused at the parallel, or at least the fact that you observed the correlation and view your union in such a hallowed light.

**Situation:** You and your prospect, a former girlfriend, are thinking about getting back together.

**Mr. Inhibited:** "I think we should."

**Hog:** (triumphantly) "Once they've had a taste of The Kid, they always want more."

**Skillful Flirt:** "We're like Richard Burton and Liz Taylor - destined to be together, no matter how tumultuously."

## When You've Been Turned Down

After being rejected, most guys either turn nasty or just walk away hurt. In fact, this is the best time to show how cool and secure you are by nonchalantly turning your rejection into a joke.

Keep in mind that an initial rejection isn't necessarily a final rejection. Many women feel the need to establish up front that they're not "easy", and once they've established that, they let their guard down. Think about the number of times you've heard some woman say she married her husband because he was so persistent.

When you first ask your prey out, and she says, "I can't," reply, "Finish the sentence please." When she asks what you mean, say, "I can't on Tuesday – but I'd love to on Wednesday."

Or just make a harsh buzzing sound, and say, "Wrong answer! Let's try that one again from the top. Now – would you like to have lunch with me sometime?"

Next time you see her, tell her, "I'm utterly exhausted." When she asks why, reply, "I've spent the past week racking my brains trying to figure out how to turn a 'no' into a 'yes'."

The next few times you see her, ask, "Change your mind?" When she says no, answer, "You will."

The next time she says no, wail, "You don't seem to be weakening at all!"

Turn it into a sort of running joke between the two of you, and after a while it'll seem as if you've become friends. Whether she eventually gives in or not, this approach will take some of the sting of rejection away.

> **Situation:** Your prospect turns you down for a date.
>
> **Mr. Inhibited:** "Oh well. I tried."
>
> **Hog:** What're you, a dyke?"
>
> **Skillful Flirt:** "It must be hard for you to keep your desire for me in check like that. I must say, I admire your will power."

## Make "Reluctant" Compliments

There's no better way to make your prospect feel foolish than to give a compliment which sounds as if it was dragged out of you, and you are just saying it to be polite. So whether she says something egotistical or genuinely self-deprecating, respond with a "compliment" in a way that makes it sound as if she had fished for it. She'll think you're only being polite, and thus will feel foolish and be eager to do something to make herself look good in your eyes again. This means you'll have her wrapped around your little finger, which is just where you want her.

Let's say she makes a mistake and comments, "Boy am I stupid!" Immediately respond, "No you're not, you're very smart." But sound vaguely bored and ever so slightly annoyed as you say it, as if this is a pro forma response which you had no choice but to give.

If she makes a lame joke, force a laugh. Don't make it so obviously forced that she thinks you're being sarcastic; just make it ever so slightly forced, so it is apparent that you're not really amused.

If she complains about her lack of success in any arena, offer the following salve: "I think you're quite successful in your own way." The "in your own way" formulation extracts any real value from the compliment, but makes you look well-mannered, and her feel condescended to.

Any "compliment" you give should be delivered in the same tone a parent uses to reassure an anxious child.

You'll be amazed at how good the reaction when you patronize someone who isn't used to being patronized, like a beautiful woman. Just be sure your motives remain invisible.

> **Situation:** Your prospect looks in the mirror and says, "My looks are really going downhill."
>
> **Mr. Inhibited:** Looks taken aback, says, "What?"
>
> **Hog:** (nodding in agreement): "Yup."
>
> **Skillful Flirt:** (sounding distracted and slightly bored): "No they're not, you're a very good-looking woman."

# Make Bets

Nothing adds to the excitement of an evening like the illicit thrill of gambling. You needn't travel all the way to Vegas, or even the local reservation, to give your prospect this thrill. All you need to do is make a series of harmless little bets with your prey, bets you're sure she will win, to create your own little Sin City.

Bet a dollar on who can keep their balance on one foot the longest.

Bet on who can throw a candy wrapper into the trash bin from the greatest distance.

Bet on who can run up a flight of stairs quicker, you (hopping on one leg) or her (using both of hers).

Turn the evening into a decathlon of sorts. Just make sure she wins most of the contests. Give her the sensation of winning money, even though you're not betting significant amounts. There's nothing like found money to put someone in a positive frame of mind, and if she's positive about the evening, she'll be positive about you.

If your prospect initially balks at the idea of gambling, make this speech: "What most people don't realize is that every choice they make in life is a bet. Which college to go to. Which career to pursue. Which guy to marry. Life is just one big gamble. What you and I are doing is very small potatoes by comparison."

To add to her thrill, act frustrated each time you lose. Say, "I didn't realize what a shark you are. Or maybe what a pigeon I am. You just roped me into all these bets without my even realizing what was going on."

If she points out that you were the one who suggested the bets, respond, "That's just what a shark does! She makes her mark think that he's the one suggesting the bets, when in fact it's the shark who's manipulated him into making the bets. Don't think I don't see what's going on. Did you ever work as a carnie?"

Once you've got her in that betting mode, she'll find that she enjoys the thrill of victory (there's a reason Gamblers Anonymous exists). She'll also feel just a little bit naughty, which will predispose her toward other kinds of thrills.

> **Situation:** You're on a date, and you've just made a dollar bet about who can chug a beer faster.
>
> **Mr. Inhibited:** Loses because he's not good at drinking beer.
>
> **Hog:** Beats her (just as he's done on every other bet so far this evening), then crows, "Ha! You weren't even close!"
>
> **Skillful Flirt:** Loses intentionally, then says, "You must be some sort of professional gambler. You roped me in like a pro!" When he suggests a rematch and she demurs, replies, "Don't tell me you're not going to give me a chance to win my money back. Now *that's* poor sportsmanship."

## If She's Hesitant

If your prospect seems reluctant to go out with you, tell her, "I don't blame you for pulling back, I'd probably be doing the same if I were you. You never know, there are a lot of weird people out there, believe me, I know from experience."

Saying this makes you seem less aggressive, and less dangerous. By saying you've had bad experiences with people too, you're subtly putting yourself on her side. And by not pushing, you also cause her to stop pulling away.

Say, 'To tell the truth, I like to take it slow too." This establishes you as the kind of guy who's more interested in serious long-term relationships than immediate sexual gratification (in other words, as one of a kind).

Underline your uniqueness by adding, "Men are always in such a hurry; to me, the whole pleasure is in getting to know someone."

"People who rush into things like this often have no idea what they're getting into. I like to get to know someone first." Falser words may never have been spoken, but she'll probably take yours at face value. Add, "Seems to me it's just the basic instinct for self-preservation."

If your prey is attractive, she's probably so used to pushy guys that you'll be a refreshing change. And showing that you're in no hurry shows that she is in no imminent danger, which means she can relax and let her guard down – which clears the way for you to pounce.

Proving yourself a woman at heart will benefit you as a man.

---

**Situation:** You've asked your prey out. She responds, "I don't know if I'm ready yet."

**Mr. Inhibited:** "Okay."

**Hog:** "You have any idea how many women would give their eyeteeth to go out with me?"

**Skillful Flirt:** "You're doing the right thing. It's always safer to get to know somebody first."

---

## "I'm Tired of Dating"

When you meet a new prospect, if she's not a party girl, you'll probably strike a responsive chord by saying, "I'm so tired of dating. Honestly, it seems like in the last couple years I've been out with fifty women, and I want it to stop. I really do. I mean, I'm just sick to death of the singles scene."

Continue, "I'm ready to settle down with someone I can build a relationship with."

Say, "All this going out on first dates, with all the awkwardness involved, the feeling that you're being graded, all the false fronts that get put up. I just want to have friends, real friends, that's all."

Then ask her out on a date thusly: "I tell you what, let's have dinner sometime. Just as friends, not like a date. Let's agree beforehand, no one makes a pass at anyone, there's no seduction involved. Just friendly conversation." This, of course, is most women's ideal first date.

It may be the opposite of your ideal date, but charm is all about pretending that your instincts are not what they are. And once you've agreed not to make a pass at her, when her guard is down, it is of course much easier to do so.

---

**Situation:** You're asking your prospect out on a first date.

**Mr. Inhibited:** "If you're not doing anything Saturday night, would you like to have dinner?"

**Hog:** "Hey, let's you and me hook up."

**Skillful Flirt:** I want to ask you out, but I don't want it to seem like a date. There's too much pressure that way. Can we just go out sometimes as friends?"

---

## The Conventional Wisdom

The old adage, "Treat a lady like a tramp and a tramp like a lady," is actually good advice, as it's always refreshing to be taken for something you're not. The only caveat is you must be absolutely sure of whom you're dealing with.

So if you know a lady whose virtue is beyond reproach (and who has demonstrated absolutely no interest in having sex with you), act as if the opposite is true. If you're absolutely sure she knows you're joking, call her "you little whore." Or "Jezebel." Or "you scarlet woman."

If she comes from an old Main Line Philadelphia family and attended a fancy finishing school, *and* if she has a relaxed sense of humor, ask, "Did you ever work as a professional?" When she looks perplexed, say, "Never mind," as if you've thought better of your question. She should get your drift.

If she has perfect manners and a genteel demeanor, ask, "Do you resent it when most guys just assume that you're an easy lay?"

If she's got a Ph.D. and teaches at a prestigious university, ask, "Have you ever worked as a stripper?" When she seems shocked that you would ask that question, quickly say, "No, I'm sorry, I didn't mean stripper, I meant *exotic dancer,*" as if her shock must have come only from your poor choice of words, not the basic thrust of your question.

On the other hand, if your prey has an aura of easy virtue about her, act as if you don't notice this and mock her for being prissy instead. Act as if you're the bad one; say, "I'm not sure how to act with you, I'm not used to Vestal Virgins." (Take care she doesn't interpret your statement as sarcasm.)

"I'm always afraid of offending someone like you who's so obviously well brought up."

"You're probably the type who's really put off when you see someone like me acting rude or crass."

If she has a certain reputation, restore her dignity by commenting, "I can tell. You're the kind of girl who maybe *thinks* about sleeping with a guy after she's been on about twenty dates with him." Then hold up your hands and say, "No thanks," as if you want no part of such a long siege.

---

**Situation:** You're talking to an upper class Englishwoman who's vacationing in the U.S.

**Mr. Inhibited:** Without realizing what he's doing, puts on a slight British accent himself.

**Hog:** "Hey, cut the bullshit phony accent, willya? Who do you think you are, Madonna?"

**Skillful Flirt:** "Let me guess what you do back in England. Don't tell me – I'm guessing you work for an escort agency. No? Wait – I've got it! You're a masseuse!"

# The Power of Alcohol

In terms of effectiveness, getting your prospect drunk is pretty much the equivalent of memorizing this entire book, then being able to execute all of its suggested routines flawlessly – while simultaneously improving upon them. Here is a rough guide to alcohol's progressive power: if your prospect has one drink, it will make you – in her eyes – a slightly more tolerable person. After two drinks, your jokes will seem wittier and your observations more insightful. After three drinks your looks will improve: all of a sudden your facial features will seem just right. After four drinks, your very character will change: you'll appear a really sweet guy with a good heart. And after five drinks, her clothes will seem unnecessary encumbrances to her.

The trick is to get her to have those drinks in the first place.

One good way to do this is to learn the names of exotic new drinks, then ask if she's tried each one. If she hasn't, and she probably won't have, insist she must because "it's all the rage in St. Tropez." Even if the drink doesn't sound appealing, the locale will. (By the way, pronounce it San Tropay, *not* Saint Tropezz, or you'll sound like a yokel.) All you need do is study the drinks menu at a trendy bar and remember a few of them. There are any number of ways to make a drink seem more appealing:

"This is what all the people in Malibu drank during those recent brush fires."

"I hear this is Orlando Bloom's favorite drink."

"You probably shouldn't have one of these 'cause they're supposed to be really addictive."

A couple cautions are in order here. First, every woman knows that a man wants to ply her with drink for one reason only, so her defenses will immediately go up. So don't ever suggest more than one drink at a time. (After a couple drinks, put her on the defensive by saying, "Don't think you're going to get me drunk just so you can take advantage of me.") Second, don't blame any subsequent bad behavior on your inebriation; most women are sophisticated enough to know that alcohol merely releases the real you.

**Situation:** You're suggesting a drink to your prospect.

**Mr. Inhibited:** "Can I buy you a drink?"

**Hog:** "Hey – let's get shit-faced!"

**Skillful Flirt:** "Have you ever tried a Dark and Stormy? I hear this is what they serve at the door to the Oscars to insure a happy audience."

## "I Feel It's Only Fair to Warn You…"

You're at your prospect's apartment and she's just offered you a drink. What do you say?

"I should warn you, I have this little problem with drinking. Just one drink and I go totally out of control. I'm like Kim Basinger in that movie *Blind Date.* I just become a maniac."

Your prospect will undoubtedly ask what you mean by that. Play coy for a little bit ("I just go crazy"). Then admit, "Well, one time three years ago after a couple drinks I evidently tried to kiss a girl." Shrug, "I told you, I become an absolute maniac."

At this point, your prospect will realize you're joking, so continue, "Under most circumstances I'm pretty normal. At least I think I am. But they say that when you drink your real personality emerges. This worries me. Am I really the kind of pervert who'll actually try to kiss a girl?"

"The other thing that concerns me is that after I've had just one drink, my memory turns off. The next day, I can never remember a thing about what happened the night before. If I have this drink, will you promise to tell me later what happened? Honestly?"

"Have you ever known anyone else who, after just one drop of alcohol, just turns into a complete animal?"

If, by this point, your prospect has not withdrawn her offer of a drink, you have pretty much carte blanche to act as you please – with her tacit approval. After all, you warned her. And afterwards, you can always claim you don't remember.

> **Situation:** You prospect offers you a beer.
>
> **Mr. Inhibited:** (knowing he needs one to relax) "Sure, thank you."
>
> **Hog:** "What kind you got? I hope not any of that cheap shit."
>
> **Skillful Flirt:** (looking concerned) "Sure, but first I should probably tell you about me and drinking…"

## "We Are Not Going to Have an Affair….."

If you want to put the idea of an affair into your prospect's head – the best way to do it is to say that you absolutely do not want to have an affair with her. Tell her you've enjoyed the friendship, and that you find her company fun, but that that's all it is. Once that seed has been sown, it should sprout into a full-fledged desire for an affair. There's never a better time to pounce than when someone's guard is down.

So add, "But now that we've agreed we're not going to have an affair, we can get together for a cup of coffee. Totally harmlessly. We can talk about our love lives."

If she's suspicious of your intentions, say, "You and I are just totally wrong for each other. But I think that we could be good friends." When she asks you why you're not suited, give a "reason" that is in fact something *she* would consider a positive: "I'm too jealous/I'm not the jealous type", or "I'm too independent/You'd probably find me too smothering," or "I'm too much of a stay-at-home type for you/I love to go out to places all the time." Pretend to be whatever she actually wants.

When you first go out with her, emphasize how much fun it is: "You know, I'm not used to having a woman just as a friend. But I have to admit, I really like it. It's so relaxing. No pressure to do anything. I can just be myself."

If she doubts you, say, "Just think of me as your gay friend. I guess that sort of makes you a fag hag. There are worse things."

There are lots of men who have offered their shoulders to cry on, then turned that role into romance.

**Situation:** Your prospect tells you she just wants to be friends.

**Mr. Inhibited:** "Okay."

**Hog:** "Come on, I'm on a hot streak. Don't ruin it for me."

**Skillful Flirt:** "Oh thank God. I was really afraid you were looking at me as something else, and I didn't want to insult you. I think romantically we're all wrong for each other. But we can still be friends. Hey, let's shake on it."

## "You Know Perfectly Well What You're Doing"

If you've fallen for your prospect, you can put her on the defensive by making it seem as if she was complicit in your "seduction". This may even fool her into thinking that she *was* complicit – and that she actually likes you.

"You know, looking back on it, I don't think you were utterly innocent as far as my falling for you."

"We're playing the game at different levels. I'm an amateur and you're a pro. I suppose those clothes that show off your charms, you just dropped into them by accident. And that walk, if you ask me, it looks a little practiced. And the way you bat your eyes....Those come hither looks....That makeup applied so artfully. It was all just an assault on my senses that I was unable to resist."

"But mostly it was the psychological manipulation, the way you'd drop those little hints, let the top of your thong ride up above your pants line. The way you'd gently touch my arm, or pull up your stockings to make sure I noticed your legs. The complimenting me on my looks, the questioning of my masculinity as a sort of challenge – it's all very calculated." (Make sure you say this lightheartedly, so it doesn't come off as Puritanical disapproval.)

> **Situation:** Your prospect acts shocked when you make a pass at her.
>
> **Mr. Inhibited:** "Sorry."
>
> **Hog:** "Come on, you know you want it."
>
> **Skillful Flirt:** (playfully) "Shocked are you? Please. You've led me by the nose every step of the way."

## "I'm Sorry – It Was an Accident"

Everyone knows that massage can have a hypnotic effect. But just lightly touching someone can exert the same effect. So brush up against your prospect and claim, jokingly, that it was an accident. If she likes you at all, she'll find your touch pleasing.

So make a joke out of it. Lightly stroke her forearm and say, "Sorry, I was just reaching for the salt."

"Oops, I was just reaching for that book."

"I was just stretching. Hey, honest accident."

Don't ever touch her private areas, just her arms, her legs, her back, her shoulders, and her hand.

Blame her: "Why do you keep getting in my way when I'm trying to do stuff?"

Emphasize any point by running a hand down her arm. Or by squeezing her hand.

If her foot is perched on a stool and is handy, reach out and give that a squeeze.

Afterwards, admit, "Well, that was just an excuse to touch you."

Or, 'Believe it or not, I'm actually doing this on purpose. You probably didn't have a clue about that."

**Situation:** You need a book which is on the other side of your prospect.

**Mr. Inhibited:** Says, "Excuse me," and stands up and goes around her to get it, giving her a wide berth.

**Hog:** "Hey, grab that book for me, willya?"

**Skillful Flirt:** Says, "Excuse me," then leans across her to get it. As he is returning to his original position, stops for a second while their faces are a few inches apart and just stares directly into her eyes. Says, "In case you couldn't guess, the only reason I reached for that book was so I could put my face close to yours."

## "I'm About to Lose My Looks"

If you want to remind your prospect that her youth and beauty are fleeting, tell her that you're at the end of your tether as far as your own looks (without sounding as if you're too taken with them):

"What little looks I have are about to disappear, swallowed up in a mass of fat and wrinkles, so you better move quickly if you want to take advantage." This will make her think about the built in obsolescence of her own beauty.

This may or may not be true – some of us lose our looks at 23, some at 50, some not until 70 (if we've had a little help), and of course most of us were never all that attractive to begin with. But everyone worries that their looks are about to go downhill, and it is certainly true that people as a rule don't get *better* looking after the age of 25. So remind your prospect – indirectly – that she should take advantage of her own youth while she still has it.

If you can, project a certain doomed quality to your life: "I feel as if I'm in the last days of my youth." The "last days" has a certain romantic sound to it, as in "the last days of Pompeii", and we all know what we'd do if we actually knew ahead of time that the world was going to end the next day – we'd run around crazily screwing our brains out. So subtly encourage that attitude in your prospect by invoking the end of an era.

"I feel as if I'm at the end of an era. In a few more years my stomach will be out to here, the skin on my face will all be around a quarter inch lower, and my hair will consist of little gray tufts around my ears. You probably won't even recognize me. The rise and fall of Nick. My glory years were ever so brief. And the worst part is, they weren't even that glorious – ignominious might be a better word. But even that is coming to a close."

> **Situation:** The subject of age arises.
>
> **Mr. Inhibited:** "Oh well, you're only as old as you feel."
>
> **Hog:** "You shoulda seen me a few years ago, I was in unbelievable shape."
>
> **Skillful Flirt:** I feel as if I'm standing at the edge of a very tall cliff, looking down at where I'm going to be in a couple years, mourning my lost youth. Hey – if you want to get me while I'm still hot, better act quickly. Okay, okay – I'm only lukewarm – but at least that's better than what I'm going to be."

## How to Respond to Being Called a Womanizer

Complete denial is the only route to take here, otherwise your prospect will see herself as just one more conquest, not a role anyone aspires to.

"I'd be a pretty poor excuse for a womanizer."

"If you only knew how thin my resume actually is."

"You're either thinking of the wrong guy, or you've been listening to someone who is a poor judge of character."

"I suppose I've dated a fair number of girls, but I've never had a bad breakup."

"If anyone were to write a book, 'The Romantic Adventures of [your name]', it wouldn't even fill one page."

"Well, I suppose I'd rather be accused of being a womanizer than what I'm usually accused of, which is being gay." Say this in a tone of helpless resignation which makes it clear neither accusation is true.

Or express desire: "I wish" or "In my dreams".

Or express confusion: "Aren't womanizers guys who have lots of short term girlfriends? Just about all I've ever had are long term girlfriends."

Or, "Really, I'm more of a woman than a womanizer. I'm not gay, but for some reason I just identify with women more."

> **Situation:** Your prospect says she hears you're a womanizer.
>
> **Mr. Inhibited:** "Me?!"
>
> **Hog:** "Yes, and a very successful one too I might add."
>
> **Skillful Flirt:** "I think my numbers would have to be a lot higher for me to qualify as that. I'm into quality, not quantity." Stares at her directly, so that she gets the message that *she* represents quality.

## If You're Accused of Insincerity

At some point during a courtship, a woman is likely to say, "Oh, I'll bet you tell that to all the girls," or question your sincerity in some other way. At that point, whether or not you are sincere, you must demonstrate that you are. Here are several ways to "prove" your statements were in fact heartfelt. Pick any two or three of the following:

First, stumble by choking on your words so something unintelligible comes out, then say, "See? I was at a complete loss for words – does that seem like what would happen to a glib liar?"

Or simply say, "I've never meant anything more sincerely in my life."

"I tell you what, I'll take a lie detector test if you don't believe me. You name the time and place, I'll be there." (This is the ultimate grandstand offer: she'd never track down a lie detector expert and pay him to hook you up.)

"What can I possibly do to prove to you I'm telling the truth?" If she asks you to do something ridiculous, like pay her a lot of money or jump off a bridge, say, "How would that prove I was telling the truth? If anything, that would show that I was lying, otherwise I wouldn't do something so desperate."

"Anyway, if you're so cynical you don't believe me, that's sort of sad. I don't know what life experiences you've had to make you that way, but….it's just sad."

Or just sound slightly angry and say, "You know what? I don't care if you don't believe me. I know I'm telling the truth, and that's all that matters." (These don't sound like the words of a liar.)

> **Situation:** You tell your prospect you have an insane crush on her, and she replies, "That sounds like a well-used line to me."
>
> **Mr. Inhibited:** "It's not – really -- it's not!"
>
> **Hog:** "Lines? Believe me, I got a lotta good ones. A *lot*."
>
> **Skillful Flirt:** "I do occasionally lie. Everyone does, when they're forced to. But when I do, people rarely doubt me, and what's ironic is, this time I'm telling the truth, and you don't believe me."

## "It's Dark Out There"

Should your prospect be at your apartment and the hour late, it's incumbent upon you to invent reasons why she not venture into the night. (If you're at her apartment, use them for yourself.)

Say, "You don't want to deal with all the drunk drivers out there now. I'd never forgive myself if something happened to you."

If she's had just one drink herself, no matter how weak or how long ago, take her car keys from her and say self-righteously, "Friends don't let friends drive drunk."

Say, "I'd offer to escort you back myself, but the fact is, I'm afraid of the dark, and if you had any sense, you would be, too."

"Why would you want the bogeyman to get you? Didn't your mother ever tell you about how he comes out at night?"

"This is when the most crimes are committed, under cover of darkness. Look at any police blotter, you'll see what I'm talking about."

"You've heard of the New Canaan Strangler, haven't you? He's our local serial killer. He always does his raping and murdering when it gets dark outside." (Makes sure she knows you're kidding.) "Believe me, you're much safer here with me."

Most girls will respond to this by saying, "I'm not sure I am." Reply, "Of course you are. Look, you can have my bed. I'll take the couch." (This scenario may be as unlikely as the supposed serial killer in your town, but give her a big fake-honest look as you say it.)

Add, "I'll even loan you my extra set of pj's. I just washed them the other day. We can have a pajama party!" (There's something innocent about a pajama party, and the fact that the phrase is on the tip of your tongue makes it seem as if you come from a sheltered background, which makes you a little less scary. She won't take your offer seriously, but she may relax a bit.)

Conclude, "The problem is, if you left now, and anybody saw you, they'd get the wrong impression. Why not just wait until morning, and then people will just think, 'Oh, she just went over there for breakfast. It was totally innocent'." (This is of course completely absurd, but once it gets dark, people get tired, and giddiness reigns.)

The best you can hope for with these types of lines is that your prospect plays along with your game, and pretends fear of the dark – which will at least give her a nominal excuse to stay. If she doesn't play it this way, well, at least the two of you have had a chuckle.

> **Situation:** Your prospect tells you it's time for her to leave.
>
> **Mr. Inhibited:** "Oh, let me walk you to your car."
>
> **Hog:** "C'mon, you gotta be kidding me, it's early – we haven't even had any fun yet! You know what I'm talking about."
>
> **Skillful Flirt:** "Are you crazy! You can't go out now -- this is when the werewolves come out!"

# How to Compliment a Sexual Performance

For a man, this task is fairly simple. All you need to say afterward is, "Wow! You have a perfect body!" Just about any woman will respond to this by citing some flaw of hers, real or imagined (probably real). Pooh pooh her self-criticism by saying, "Nonsense! It's beautiful! I like it just like that."

Luckily, the de gustibus rule applies here, so she may not question your credibility. Saying this pretty much guarantees yourself a return trip.

You needn't go on about each individual body part, it sounds both a little perverse and a little dirty; but a general comment like, "Hmm, I have to say, all the little details of your body are just to my liking" strikes just the right tone.

Another comment sure to please is, "Most girls I get tired of after a short while, but I honestly can't imagine ever getting tired of you."

Adding, "I certainly hope we can do this again" will go a long way towards reassuring the woman that you are not regarding her in the harsh post-coital light which seems to affect many men's vision.

Women aren't generally as sensitive about their skill level, so you needn't dwell on that. In fact, if you go on too long about their "obvious experience" you might leave a woman feeling like a Jezebel, so sometimes it's best to leave that alone.

---

**Situation:** You've just finished up with your prospect (who has now graduated to the status of a conquest) in bed. What do you say?

**Mr. Inhibited:** "Thank you, I guess. Wow, I feel so...*relaxed* now."

**Hog:** "You ever think about getting on a Stair Master?"

**Skillful Flirt:** "You're one of the few women whose body looks better out of clothes than in them. I've got to be the luckiest guy in the world, to be with you."

# Afterword

No seduction can really be considered skillfully executed unless
it is accompanied by artful flirting. Utilizing the full repertoire means
combining flattery with mock insults, and self-deprecation with the
kind of boasting which highlights your strengths in a self-mocking way.
Compliment your prospect but at the same time keep him off-balance.
Assuming that your beau has a long and willing line of "victims" will
stroke his ego in such a way as to give him the confidence to make
another "victim" out of you. Alternatively, you can pretend he has
no effect on you at all, as a sort of challenge. You can either exaggerate
or (playfully) demean his masculinity to goad him into action as well.
Very few men will not be tickled by these techniques. On the other hand,
a woman should be handled differently, since they usually prefer romance
in the mix. For many women, the ideal man thinks more like a woman, so
she should be wooed with more "heartfelt" sentiments, not the type of
joking men tend to enjoy among themselves. So make sure that your
overtures make her feel you are smitten with her, and her alone, even if
humorous banter is your preferred approach. This is not to say there's
no place for humor: on the contrary, if you can keep your target in
constant laughter, she will enjoy your company and eventually be more
receptive to your advances when you try to get intimate with her.
And always remember, banter is good, but only when your target is
in a playful mood. (If she's not, you'll come across lame.) But if she is, a
good time will be had by all – and maybe an even better time later on.

www.ingramcontent.com/pod-product-compliance
Lightning Source LLC
Chambersburg PA
CBHW020418290526
45785CB00002B/623